PERSPECTIVES ON MANAGERIAL MARKETING

THEORY AND PRACTICE

Perspectives on Managerial Marketing

Theory and Practice

Editors
M. Thomas
Raju Patel

2007

CYBER TECH PUBLICATIONS
4264/3 Ansari Road, Daryaganj, New Delhi - 110 002

Perspectives on Managerial Marketing: Theory and Practice

First Edition 2007

Published by G.S. Rawat
For Cyber Tech Publications
4264/3, Ansari Road, Daryaganj, New Delhi - 110 002
E-mail : cybertechpublishers@yahoo.com
Phone : 011-23244078,
Fax : 011-23280028

...t Press, Moujpur, # 9810878184

PREFACE

Marketing as a field of study is generally categorized as being part of the broader field of business administration. However, marketing also involves considerations that extend beyond these boundaries. Marketing decisions are shaped by and influence the external environments of the firm. Marketing, therefore, has social, economic, legal, international, and political dimensions in addition to its managerial focus. Profitable solutions to marketing problems can only be realized if the significance of environmental change on the firm and its customers is recognized. These external forces which affect consumer behaviour and business action must be reflected in marketing policies, plans, programmes, and decisions.

The student of marketing must develop a facility for integrating useful contributions from many disciplines. He must also understand the functional purpose of each component in a marketing action system.

Different sources scholars and institutions for their valuable contribution on this subject. While preparing this work for our readers.

Last but not the least my publishers who appreciated this book and brought this work out in a record time.

– Editors

CONTENTS

1

INTRODUCTION

This introductory section outlines the structure and organization of the book, the major topics covered in managerial marketing, and the nature of interrelationships among diverse aspects of marketing management. Among the areas discussed are: the systems approach to marketing, marketing management, the role of consumers and consumer behaviour, the managerial functions of marketing, decision strategies and techniques, and the marketing mix. Some new broader dimensions influencing the marketing manager's job are also presented, including recent developments in international marketing and management's increasing concern with the social responsibility of the firm. These marketing developments are receiving increased consideration because their effect on marketing success is now more widely recognized.

Marketing as a field of study is generally categorized as being part of the broader field of business administration. However, marketing also involves considerations that extend beyond these boundaries. Marketing decisions are shaped by and influence the external environments of the firm. Marketing, therefore, has social, economic, legal, international, and political dimensions in addition to its managerial focus. Profitable solutions to marketing problems can only be realized if the significance of environmental change on the firm and its customers is recognized. These external forces which affect consumer behaviour and business action must be reflected in marketing policies, plans, programmes, and decisions.

The student of marketing must develop a facility for integrating useful contributions from many disciplines. He must also understand the functional purpose of each component in a marketing action system. Illustration I depicts a total marketing system and services as a model for the study of marketing management. The conceptual relationships portrayed are developed in subsequent illustrations and readings. This marketing systems model is presented in the spirit of the following passage from Konrad Lorenz:[1]

I am aware that the task I have set myself makes excessive demands upon my pen. It is almost impossible to portray in words the functioning of a system in which every part is related to every other in such a way that each has a causal influence on the others. Even if one is only trying to explain a gasoline engine it is hard to know where to begin, because the person to whom one seeks to explain it can only understand the nature of the crankshaft if he has first grasped that of the connecting rods, the pistons, the valves, the camshaft, and so on. Unless one understands the elements of a complete system as a whole, one cannot understand them at all. The more complex the structure of a system is, the greater this difficulty becomes—and it must be surmounted both in one's research and in one's teaching. Unfortunately the working structure of the instinctive and culturally acquired patterns of behaviour which make up the social life of man seems to be one of the most complicated systems we know on this earth.

The External Environments of Marketing

Marketing managers, by the nature of their problems, are environmentalists. They give attention to the implications of environmental changes for marketing policies and practices. Illustration I shows the external environment in which the systemic functions of marketing are managed. These environments and interactions affect marketing opportunities, customer behaviour and satisfaction, and the degree of success achieved by the business.

In this model, the major external environmental influences on business actions are categorized as: scientific and technological forces; life style and life space forces; ethical, legal, and social forces; and both domestic and international economic and political forces. Each of these forces interacts with the corporate system. Their impact on marketing management is investigated in further chapters.

The marketing manager needs to appreciate the pervasive influence of these forces on consumer attitudes and behaviour. While the activities of any single business cannot appreciably alter any of the external forces, the converse relationship exists – any one force can affect business outcome. Customers react to and help shape their environments, and market opportunities or problems result from changed customer attitudes toward products and services.

Three linkage levels involved in the analysis of marketing systems are shown in the model.

1. Marketing activities are linked through the corporate enterprise system to the various public and private agencies external to the firm. Examples of these agencies, which are not depicted in the model, include: suppliers; advertising firms and media; financial institutions; governmental and private research organisations; federal, state, and local governmental commissions; transportation companies; and the various publics.

2. Linkages exist between marketing and the other business functions that comprise the corporate enterprise system. These other areas are represented by the firm's human, physical, and financial resources, its competitive structure, and its goals. Because the purpose of this model is depiction of a marketing action system, other functional areas of the business have not been explicitly differentiated. Similar models could be constructed for production, finance, and other functions of an enterprise.

3. The systemic functions of marketing are linked to produce

an effective marketing-customer satisfactions mix. Three sub-mixes—product-services, communications, and distribution—are combined to achieve marketing objectives. The objective of the marketing mix is to balance marketing objectives. The objective of the marketing mix is to balance marketing effort with marketing opportunity in order to provide optimal marketing support of stated corporate goals.

The nature of marketing operations within the corporate enterprise system, and emphasizes that corporate goals are achieved by concentrating on defined areas of market opportunity or, more precisely, on customers in particular market segments. Corporate goal setting is recognized today as a complex process for conglomerate, multinational, multi-plant firms.

The Consumer

Chapter three deals with the consumer, the focal point of marketing effort. The consumer, by his decision to buy or not buy a product, holds veto power over the firm's entire marketing and business effort. Many of the elements that influence consumer behaviour and satisfaction are considered in this chapter.

Like the others, Chapter three is future-oriented. One purpose of analyzing the articles in the book is to enable the reader to better understand and ultimately meet the problems consumers will have in the future. For example, understanding of consumer behaviour is increased by studying trends in life style and life space forces. In Chapter three, some of these trends are identified, and their impact on marketing programmes are treated in detail.

Market segmentation provides one way of identifying marketing opportunities that have arisen because of changing life styles. Broad potential markets are broken down into many smaller segments, each with its own tastes, preferences, values, and needs.

The market segmentation concept is the basis of a marketing strategy directed toward consumers with particular life styles and needs. While demographic methods are basic, other criteria for market segmentation are also useful. Examples of newer methods of segmentation analysis include the determination of differences in buyer attitudes, motivations, values, patterns of usage, and aesthetic preferences.

Consumer motivation is a function of the extent to which human needs are satisfied. One theory of human motivation holds that needs are satisfied. One theory of human motivation holds that needs are arranged on a continuum that ranges from basic physiological needs to those of self-actualisation.[2] An appreciable measure of satisfaction of lower needs is a precondition for emergence of higher ones. The marketing manager's task to is to assemble a market offer that promises gratification of at least one level in this hierarchy of needs.

Consumer behaviour is influenced by the life style ad life space force discussed in this book. Many marketing efforts of American business and many of the changes taking place in consumption cannot be understood unless life style trends are considered.

There seems to be an increasing worldwide interest in personal achievement, social goals, and a better way of life. This has been described as the "revolution of rising expectations" and seems to be worldwide. For example, throughout the world there is an upward mobility thrust toward more education and more real income. The above trends are especially evident in the United States. Trends toward home entertainment and family-centered enjoyment are related to increasing discretionary time and mobility. Changes in the geographic distribution of the population are reflected in a redistribution of the labour force and purchasing power.

Tomorrow's customers may have problems that are quite unlike the buying and consumption problems prevalent today. Future consumers will generally be better educated, have greater mobility, possess more discretionary income, and have more time to spend that income. Hopefully, new communication and distribution patterns will lead to increasingly informed decisions and prompt satisfaction of consumer wants.

Decision Making in Marketing

The articles in Chapter four deal with marketing as a prime focus of managerial decision making. Marketing management is becoming increasingly analytical as models and techniques for information gathering and problem solving are developed, and as new marketing applications of existing scientific methods are discovered. Scientific and technological developments are having a continuing impact on the advancement of science in marketing. For example, the computer is exerting a significant influence on such areas as marketing planning, the evaluation of promotional alternatives, and distribution systems. Some authorities see marketing as the great growth area of computer applications in business. The rapid accumulation of new knowledge is resulting in widespread application of mathematical, statistical, economic, psychological, and sociological techniques to marketing problems. These interdisciplinary contributions to marketing promise better understanding of complex consumer needs and of other marketing problems.

Marketing Management Functions

The functions of marketing management identified in the upper center discussed in further chapters. The functions are marketing opportunity assessment, marketing planning and programming, marketing organization and leadership, and evaluating and adjusting marketing effort. The marketing management team must perform these four entrepreneurial functions if the firm is to develop an efficient corporate marketing system in a changing environment.

Marketing opportunity assessment centers on the delineation of actual and potential customers and their wants and needs. Market opportunity exists when a business either possesses or can develop capabilities that enable it to profitably satisfy the wants of potential customers. The business must continually develop marketing strategies that will enable I to cultivate these market opportunities.

Research and development activities of business, government, and educational institutions are resulting in increasing numbers of new consumer and industrial products. Similarly, increased productivity resulting from automation and other forces has resulted in production capacity that enables most manufacturing firms to produce more than they can sell. The mass production capability of American industry is predicated on the discovery of new markets and the expansion of existing ones. This is one of the factors underlying the marketing orientation of American business.

Planning is essential to the organization, operation, and control of a business. Planning also provides a basis for an integrated systems orientation and a coordinated marketing strategy. The development of new products and new markets raises organizational and leadership problems for marketing management. The interaction that occurs between an organisation and its environment illustrates the dynamics of the systems approach and reflects the demands being placed on the marketing organization and its leadership.

Evaluating and adjusting the marketing effort enables the firm to react to changes occurring in the environment. The process of change—and the ability to cope with it -is a major challenge to marketing management. Financial and integrative controls are used to keep the marketing effort keyed to areas of profitable market opportunity.

Managing the Marketing Mix

The lower central section provide an overview of the dimensions and complexities of developing and managing a marketing mix. Preparing an effective marketing mix that furthers attainment of corporate objectives is the marketing manager's responsibility.

A marketing mix consists of three sub mixes—the product and service mix, the communications mix, and the distribution mix. The product and services mix is composed of elements that form the set of utilities a customer buys. Examples of utility set contents include the product, price, services, container, brand, label information, conditions of sale, and warranty. A communications mix consists of the firm's efforts to disseminate information about its market offer to the potential byrs. The elements of a communications mix are advertising, sales promotion, personal selling, merchandising, and special sales aids. The distribution mix I formed of two major components—channels of distribution through which goods and titles to goods flow from the firm to the ultimate purchasers, and physical distribution, which is concerned with loading, transporting, storing, and delivering the product.

The marketing manager's responsibility for formulating an effective mix and for putting it into practice does not culminate with the sale of the product or service. He must not neglect the post-transactional ingredients of his marketing mix if the firm's long-range marketing strategy is to be successful.

International Marketing

The external environmental areas of domestic and international economic and political forces. The evolution of international markets is one of the most significant trends in contemporary marketing. Further chapters presents an international view of marketing and the development of the multinational firm.

Many of the forces described in the book are related to the United States market. However, their impact in the United States Portends changes of a similar nature in many countries throughout the world. For example, the knowledge explosion, particularly in science and technology, is influencing nearly all cultures. New marketing opportunities are presented by widespread rising consumption expectations and increased interest in personal achievement and social gains. Political unrest in newly formed nations around the world reflects, at lest in part, dissatisfaction with present living standards. These people want, and intend to obtain for themselves, those goods now enjoyed by consumers in more advanced economies. Similarly, some nations with controlled economies seem to be moving from a production to a partial consumer orientation. The marketing knowledge and ability possessed by multinational firms can aid immensely in the development of balanced economies in both new and changing political-economic systems. Marketing managers must recognize, analyze, and adjust to the marketing systems of each international market. Attempts to improve the efficiency of these marketing systems must be based on a thorough evaluation of the system's socio-political environment.

Marketing plays a key role in the economic growth of developing countries. To the extent that the socioeconomic growth of a nation is related to the marketing process, marketing can be a critical element in the development process. Marketing is not only an economic tool, but a political and social tool as well. Ultimately, marketing's most important social role may lie in its contribution to the stimulation and facilitation of world peace.

Societal and Interdisciplinary Dimensions of Marketing

Marketing practitioners and academicians realize that various ethical, legal, social, economic, and political forces are becoming increasingly important for marketing Illustration I identifies these forces as major influences on markets. Their effects on marketing thought and action are discussed in this book.

The socioeconomic dimensions of marketing account, in part, for the growing concern of business and marketing leaders with public and private views of social responsibility in business. Te continuing emphasis on the need for businesses to increase their efforts to fulfill their assigned citizenship roles reflects an expanding concept of business' social responsibility.

In order to fully understand marketing's dynamics and the changes in marketing described in this book, students and managers must not only understand problem-solving techniques, they must also understand the theory underlying these techniques and practices. Some developments that influence marketing as a discipline, the interdisciplinary approach to marketing, and the contributions of theory to marketing management are explored in this book.

The articles included in the book were chosen for their contribution to an understanding of managerial marketing. The perspective throughout is that marketing managers must equip themselves to better understand the problems of potential customers and, ultimately, to help customers satisfy their requirements in a manner that meets the needs not only of customer and firm but also of society.

REFERENCES

1. Konrad Lorenz, *On Aggression* (New York: Harcourt, Brace & World, Inc., 1966), p. xi.

2. A.H. Maslow, *Motivation and Personality* (New York: Harper & Row, Publishers, 1954), pp. 80-106.

2

THE MARKETING MANAGEMENT CONCEPT

Peter Drucker has written that it is marketing that distinguishes business from other forms of organization. This statement is based on his view that the purpose of a business is to create a customer. A firm that sees its basic purpose in such terms inevitably recognizes the importance of marketing. Decisions concerning marketing questions frequently go well beyond the functional limits of an organisation's marketing system. This is why many of the topics in this book are of interest to non-marketing executives. Marketing activities interact with research and development, production, finance, procurement, and personnel functions. Decisions in one are often influence one or more other functions of the firm.

Marketing Management and Business Policy

Marketing is such an integral part of the study and practice of business administration that it cannot be logically separated from the basic questions of business strategy and policy. This is the underlying rationale for the systems approach to marketing management, which will be explained in the next section. As a result, one of the interesting trends in policy-making today is top management's recognition that the study of broad business policy issues cannot be fruitfully pursued without an understanding of the close relationship between marketing considerations and corporate policy.

From a social point of view, the future development of a free society depends in substantial measure on progress in the marketing area. In the United States economy, mass distribution faces the challenge of matching the technical excellence of mass production. Economies cannot enjoy the benefits of mass production without efficient marketing systems. This is as true in Russia as it is in the United States. An automated economy produces only filled warehouses and clogged pipelines unless marketing progress is made. The problem of facilitating distribution progress now confronts marketing managers. It can be met only if the pivotal role of modern marketing in our economy is understood and appreciated and marketing factors are related directly to company decisions.

When the marketing concept is accepted as a matter of corporate philosophy, marketing becomes the basis for designing total systems of business action. Fundamental strategies of the business are conceived and implemented on the basis of market needs, forces, and opportunities. Marketing then becomes a way of corporate life and a philosophy of business organisation and operation, with the ultimate purpose of helping consumers solve diverse consumption problems in ways compatible with the profit position and objectives of the firm.[1]

A major marketing management task is that of adapting to market opportunity through planned innovation. Planned innovation is a basic characteristic of the modern marketing concept. Innovation based on programmed research and development is now standard competitive procedure; in act, it has become a necessity if a firm is to survive and grow. Planned marketing involves both adjusting to the innovations of competitors and providing creative counter innovation by the firm.

It is likely that in the future more firms will accept the point view that innovation and change are fundamental considerations formulating marketing policy. In a dynamic marketing climate, the marketing manager must take on, as a first order of business, the task of developing and implementing strategy that will overcome resistance to change. As this occurs, research and development will become more integral parts of the marketing function.

Fred Borch, president of General Electric Company, pointed out that understanding modern marketing rests on two key fundamentals – the "dual-core" job of marketing and the profit, rather that, the volume, concept. These two key fundamentals are described below.[2]

Dual Core Marketing Job

The initial part of the dual-core job is that marketing management must focus business effort on the customer's needs and desires, including those needs and desires the customer is *not* aware of, as well as those he recognizes. Only after identification of these needs can marketing people guide the firm in determining what each function of the business should do to provide the necessary products and services to satisfy customers. The other half of the dual-core job of marketing is a more familiar one – namely, the need to persuade the prospective customer, through all the arts of selling and advertising, to purchase the products and services that have been developed.

The Profit Concept

The second fundamental on which the modern marketing philosophy rests, according to Borch, is the profit concept, not the volume concept. Volume is not eliminated as a rewarding way of obtaining profits; rather, Borch is referring to the profitless volume or volume-for-the-sake-of-volume-alone concept.

His position, which has been accepted widely, is that marketing is essentially a philosophy of business operation and not merely a function of business. Basic to this philosophy is the acceptance of a customer-oriented way of doing business. "Under marketing, the customer becomes the fulcrum, the pivot point about which the business moves in operating for the balanced best interests of all concerned."

This is not to suggest that marketing is necessarily more important as a business function than production or finance. Manufacturing, marketing, and other business functions are complementary components of the total business process. But, it is now recognized that marketing factors must be considered before physical production begins. In an advanced economy such as that of the United States, where consumer considerations are dominant, producing a market is at least of equal significance to producing a product. As Drury has pointed out: "The making and the marketing of goods are becoming so interwoven they are being recognized and practiced for what they have always been in theory—complementary parts of the productive process. Engineering know-how produces the workable know-how; marketing know-how produces a salable product."[3]

In short, ample justification exists for acceptance of the marketing management concept. The essence of this justification is contained in three points noted by Wroe Alderson:

1. The American Economy is a market-oriented economy.
2. It is essential that the top management of successful companies consist f market-oriented executives.
3. top management executives who accept the marketing concept must rely on marketing executives who are knowing and skillful users of marketing techniques, analyses and planning....[4]

These three points are still basic; the question is how best to implement them. In summary, the relationship of the marketing concept to the corporate enterprise system and to responsible executive action involves:

1. Market offerings in accordance with actual and potential consumer demand.
2. Continuous monitoring of market offerings to relate them more adequately to customer wants and needs.
3. Continuous feedback of marketing intelligence to determine existing or predicted imbalances and thus delineate market opportunities for managerial consideration.

4. The integration and coordination of resources to achieve a total system of action.

Marketing Management and the Consumer

The two essential missions of marketing management in a firm are: (1) to mobilize and direct market-related resources of the enterprise to capitalize on market opportunities by serving consumer wants and needs; (2) to help imbue company management and employees with the consumer orientation to business action. The consumer is thus the focal point around which marketing, and ultimately all business activity, revolves. The consumer orientation to business decision making is fundamental to the marketing concept. It is the key to understanding the marketing management concepts presented in this book.

In practice, marketing problems are often considered from the point of view of an industry, a manufacturer, a middleman, or a governmental unit. As a result, they are viewed from the wrong problem-solving perspective, because the primacy of the consumer is misunderstood. With a consumer orientation to business, market-related problems are appraised as customer and consumer problems rather than as corporate or functional problems.

In essence, the business enterprise is governed largely by consumer sovereignty rather than by authoritarianism of either corporate management for the government. Accepting the point of view that the consumer is king implies a recognition of the freedom of consumer choice and the voluntary action that underlies achievement of market goals. A Consumer-oriented company is one in which the total resources of the firm are attuned to existing and potential areas of profitable market opportunity. Since the concept of consumer satisfaction is so important to the marketing philosophy, the scientific study of consumers is central to the development of marketing strategy.

A research-based method of solving marketing problems is a cornerstone of the marketing management concept. Up-to-date information about consumers and consumer behaviour is pivotal to the effective mobilization of marketing resources. A growing recognition of the importance of investigating and understanding the complexities of consumer behaviour is evidenced in contemporary research projects and the growing use of the interdisciplinary approach in solving marketing problems.

With the application of automation and the resulting increase in rate of productivity, and with more efficient use of marketing resources, standards of living should substantially increase in the future. Part of this higher standard of living will be reflected in the increased amount of leisure time available to consumers. Questions can be raised concerning the role of marketing in an economy of increased abundance and discretionary time. For example, will marketing become a significant force in extending and broadening cultural horizons, or will a major opportunity facing marketing be unattended?

The essential physical needs of the United States population—food, shelter, and clothing—are largely being satisfied. Marketing problems must be viewed against a background of abundance rather than against the former conditions of relative scarcity. New markets must be found in terms of types of food, types of shelter, types of clothing, and types of recreation. An opportunity for upgrading consumers' tastes and aspirations exists. Marketing can become a significant cultural and civilizing force.

It has been suggested that the next frontier for marketing is an inner one—the market of the mind and the personal development of consumers. One of the roles of marketing in the future may be that of encouraging increasing expenditures of both dollars and time for the intellectual and social development of the consumer. Marketing, during a period of increasing leisure, may well become a significant cultural force. It may provide the impetus for an improvement of consumer tastes and an increase in their cognizance and appreciation of aesthetic values. Thus, besides merely providing the economic base necessary to support the physically productive capacities, marketing ma also provide a stimulating force for the cultural development of society.

In summary, the marketing concept in application involves the following 10 elements:

1. The development of an integrated system of marketing action.
2. Appreciation and understanding of the consumer's strategic position as it shapes and determines the firm's survival and growth.
3. Acceptance of the fact that marketing activity can be planned, and that corporate destines can, to a large extent, be shaped by marketing management effort.
4. Short-and long-range planning of company activities on a regular basis, and the development of consistent strategies and tactics, resulting in an integrated system of marketing action, are seen as key management responsibilities.
5. Recognition of intra-and interdepartmental implications of marketing decisions and actions of various organizational units.
6. Programmed process and product innovation, including the development of a climate that encourages innovation, is accepted as standard and necessary.
7. Recognition of the significant role of marketing intelligence in establishing goals and targets. Market potentials become guides to corporate action.
8. Emphasis on new-product development and its impact on company profits and posture.
9. The adoption of a marketing focus in coordinating company effort, and in establishing corporate and departmental objectives consistent with achieving the firm's profit goals.
10. Reshaping company products, services, and activities to more effectively meet the demands and opportunities of the marketplace.

Some of the problems and difficulties of applying the above elements are considered in the selections in this book.[5]

REFERENCES

1. For a discussion of some of the changing parameters of marketing management, see William Lazer, "Changing Dimensions in Marketing," *The Business Quarterly*, Spring, 1959, pp. 24-27.

2. See Fred J. Borch, "The Marketing Philosophy as a Way of Business Life," *Marketing Series* No. 99, American Management Association, 1957.

3. See James G. Drury, "Is Your Problem Overproduction—or Underproduction of Markets?" Printers' Ink, July 5, 1957, pp.19-22, 58.

4. See Wroe Alderson, "Advancing Marketing Efficiency," from the *Proceedings of the 41st National Conference of the American Marketing Association*, December, 1958.

5. For a discussion of the relationship between the marketing concept and the managerial functions of marketing, see Eugene J. Keley, *Marketing: Strategies and Functions*, (Englewood Cliffs, N.J.: Prentice-Hall, Inc., 1965).

3

THE SYSTEMS APPROACH TO MARKETING

Marketing System Defined

The marketing management philosophy is based on a systems perspective of decision-making. The systems approach to marketing has already had a substantial impact on the development of marketing thought and the management of marketing activity. This approach provides a conceptual framework for market planning, determination of the marketing mix, physical distribution, and the use of operations research techniques in marketing. Systems thinking recognizes the interrelations and inter-connections among the components of a marketing system.

The systems approach is based n the work of Von Bertalanffy, who is credited with coining the phrase "general systems theory." He defined a system as a set of objects together with the relationships among them and their attributes.[1]

Marketing institutions and operations can be perceived as complex, large-scale systems. For analytical purposes any group of marketing elements and activities that can be physically or conceptually delineated is a marketing system. A system is a collection of entities that can be understood as forming a coherent group. The fact that the entities can be defined as a coherent group is what differentiates a system from a meaningless collection of parts.[2]

In marketing systems, there are flows of products, services, money, equipment, and information. It is these flows that largely determine the survival and growth capacities of a firm. The systems approach places great emphasis on the analysis of flows and communications. It stresses the development of communication systems for transmitting information about changing market environments and subsequent adjustments of marketing policies and strategies.

Elements of Marketing Systems

Marketing systems include the following components:

1. A set of functionally interdependent marketing relationship among people and institutions in the system—manufacturers, wholesalers, retailers, facilitating agencies, and consumers.
2. Interaction between individuals and firms to maintain relationships, and facilitate adjustment to change, innovation, cooperation, and competition.
3. Establishment of objectives, goals, targets, beliefs, symbols, and sentiments that evolve from and reinforce the interaction, thus producing realistic marketing objectives and programmes, and creating favorable images, attitudes, and opinions.
4. A consumer-oriented environment within which interactions take place, subject to the constraints of a competitive market economy, the legal and socioeconomic environment, and the evolving relationships and methods of marketing entities.
5. Technology of marketing, including communications media, credit facilities, standardization and grading, marketing research, and physical distribution.

Kinds of Marketing Systems

The operational delineation of a system depends, in part, on the dominant activity being described, i.e., whether it is a sales management system, a manufacturer-dealer system, a physical distribution system or a corporate communications system. But the systems perspective is a useful one regardless of the kind of system being delineated, since it directs analysis to the actions and reactions of the firm as it operate within its many environments.

Marketing systems maybe of two types—conceptual or physical. Most marketing systems are conceptual. However, some systems, such as physical distribution systems, are physical entities. Also, the parts of a marketing system may be within or outside the formal boundaries of the firm. Many of them extend beyond the firm. For example, a manufacturer's marketing system may well include wholesalers, retailers, financial institutions, and advertising agencies.

A marketing system as an assemblage or combination of activities, institutions, ad operations is composed of subsystems. Any marketing institutions, and operation sis composed of subsystems. Any marketing component can be explained in term of various systems. Hierarchies of subsystems exist. Marketing systems are linked to larger formal systems. The advertising department can be viewed as system, as can the marketing department, the business enterprise, or the totality of a number of business enterprises.

Marketing systems may be perceived of as small systems, middle-range systems, and large systems[3] Small systems are concerned with marketing within the firm. The marketing mix or the physical distribution system are examples. The middle-range systems are those concerned with marketing's linkage to other functional activities, such as finance and production. A good example is the credit system. The large system or macro-system is concerned with marketing's linkages among manufacturers, or manufacturers, wholesalers, and retailers. Voluntary cooperatives are large systems.

A question can be raised about the appropriate structural forms that marketing systems should take. The true test is survival and effectiveness. Certain forms and system structures are more suitable at one period of time in a market than at another. Over time, the elements of the system that are approved by the marketplace are the most appropriate.

Systems thinking – the integration and coordination of marketing activities – is providing a new perspective for solving marketing problems. Systems have become powerful interpretative marketing tools. The systems approach to marketing turns on the central theme that reality occurs in systems. "It is in systems that all forms of activity manifest themselves. Therefore, any form of activity may be produced by a suitable system."[4] This implies that the system is the master model for marketing activity.

The mathematical theory of systems analysis, based on electrical engineering, conceives of systems in terms of two complementary variables – propensities and flows. These variables apply to the understanding of systems in general.[5] The was in which they relate to different systems is indicated in Chart 1.

CHART 1

Kinds of Systems

Systems Variable	*Mechanical Systems*	*Hydraulic Systems*	*Electrical Systems*	*Traffic Systems*	*Marketing Systems*
Propensity	Velocity	Pressure	Voltage	Density	Cost or price per unit of marketing effort
Flow	Force	Flow rate	Current	Current	Sales or profit per unit

The Systems Approach

The systems approach provides a master model for marketing activity. Like other models, it is imperfect. It has the advantage of focusing attention on issues broader than those usually contained in any single aspect of marketing. It places emphasis on the inputs to the system and the outputs produced. It greatly aids in the formulation of overall marketing and corporate objectives, and the development of marketing programmes and the total marketing mix. However, the systems model of marketing and corporate objectives, and the development of marketing programmes and the total marketing mix. However, the systems model of marketing activity makes no attempt to predict or understand human behaviour. It focuses on the components of the marketing systems in terms of performance rather than understanding.[6]

What are the benefits of adopting a systems perspective? First, it provides a good basis for the logical, orderly, and coherent analysis of marketing activity. This viewpoint stresses marketing linkages inside and outside the firm. It emphasizes inputs and relates them to outputs. Systems thinking furnishes information about adaptations of systems, emphasizes changing environments, and provides a conceptual framework for control.

To a large extent, the effectiveness of marketing systems depends on having and using the right information. Markets can be understood only through the study of information—communications and messages. Systems must be adjusted to markets. Thus, the information base of a system is critical to its survival and effectiveness.

Systems and Marketing Management

The marketing management concept, with its emphasis on integration, implies a systems approach to the management of marketing effort. Marketing management includes a recognition of the interrelation and inter-connection between marketing and other business elements. It adopts a systems approach as the basis for the solution of marketing problems; it is concerned with integrated and coordinated use of marketing resources to achieve predetermined and realistic objectives in an effective manner.

In accepting total responsibility for all marketing activities, and in striving for the effective use of total resources, the marketing manager must be able to see the interrelationships between various parts of the system. This perspective is suggested by Forrester. In referring to the systems view of perceiving the firm as a dynamic whole, he states, "The company will come to be recognized not as a collection of separate functions, but as a system in which the flows of information, materials, manpower, capital equipment, and money set up forces that determine the basic tendencies toward growth, fluctuation, and decline."[7]

Systems Concepts

Four groups of concepts in general systems theory have significance for marketing systems: descriptive factors, regulation and maintenance factors, factors concerning dynamics and change, and factors related to the decline and breakdown of systems.[8]

Descriptive factors are those concepts that make important distinctions in the classification of systems, structures, elements, and processes. For example, there are open and closed systems, input—output systems, boundaries and environments, orders of interaction, interdependence and independence.

Regulation and maintenance concepts deal with the control, stabilization, and regulation of systems. They are concerned with systems stability, systems equilibrium, systems feedback, homeostasis and regulation, steady-state maintenance, and communication.

Dynamics and change are internally generated factors that deal with the response of systems to environmental conditions. They include such concepts as adaptation of a system, plasticity and elasticity of systems, learning and growth, change, dynamism and dynamics.

Decline and breakdown concepts are concerned with the disruption or breakdown of a system. Included are such factors as overload, stress, disturbance, decay, and decline.

If the integration of marketing activities is not recognized organisationally, a marketing system is not complete. However, the system need not be rigidly controlled from a central point. The components of the system can be guided by common purpose and policy without rigid control.

Two concepts are important in understanding the integrated character of the systems approach. First is the concept of synthesizing the elements and subsystems into a whole. It is concerned with integrating the abovementioned component parts into a system. Second is the concept of linkages. Linkages are the paths of connection that integrate two or more separate and distinct major or minor subsystems, each of which can function independently, to create a higher order system.

Application of the systems approach requires analysis of the elements and their functions and interactions from the point of view of individual contributions to the total system. It reflects the philosophy of the operations researcher and his perception of business as a total system of action.

Conflicting Goal Orientation

To function effectively as a system, a marketing organization should be goal directed. Unfortunately, however, the goals or objectives of marketing systems and subsystems are not always clearly specified or even compatible. It is difficult for the marketing manager to precisely define the objectives of his particular unit. To the extent that a marketing organization does not clearly specify its objectives, and is not able to co-ordinate various marketing subsystems to achieve goal-directed action, a complete systems approach has not been achieved.

In trying to achieve common goals, every business system operates through subsystems that have heir own respective goals. As a result, there are usually conflicts in any business system, and a goal tradeoff between subsystems becomes important in order to achieve greater efficiency of the overall system. Given existing or likely marketing constraints, determination of the one marketing programme that promises an optimal total marketing position becomes the major objective of a systems approach to marketing. Intra-system concessions must occur if major marketing and corporate goals are to be achieved.

Systems and Goal Models

There is a basic difference between systems and goal models—largely a difference of focus and emphasis. The goal model start with a task to be achieved and focuses directly on the use of company resources to achieve it. It implies that output is directly related to input. Doubling resources is usually equated with doubling output. The goal model, therefore, may lead to segmented perspectives and may not be the most effective model of total marketing operations.

The systems model is based on the assumption that all marketing system elements function together to achieve the objectives of the overall system, rather than the objectives of a subsystem. The starting point in the systems model is not a goal but the model of the total functioning unit. A system model is a more realistic representation of an ongoing marketing entity capable of achieving multiple goals. The systems model recognizes the multifunctional and multidimensional units involved in reaching marketing goals. It emphasizes that some resources must be allocated to non-goal-directed effort. Resources are allocated to functions involved in maintaining the marketing organisation itself. These functions include supporting marketing services and action that permits the use of effective marketing striking power. Such functions are not always directly goal-oriented.

Two inherent dangers must be recognized in using a goal model. (1) The danger that in solving problems management will adopt the perspective of one subgroup in the organisation. This is especially true when pressure exists from action-oriented marketing groups. For example, marketing managers are likely to be sales-oriented, since most marketing goals are achieved through sales. (2) The administrative, facilitating, and control functions of the marketing system may be neglected. Management must allocate resources and perform functions necessary for the maintenance of the marketing system itself.

Scope and Complexity of Marketing Systems

Marketing systems are often large and complex. For example, consider the dollar and physical volume of gods handled, the number of people employed, the number and variety of components of an advertising campaign, or the components of a sales promotion campaign in any major business concern today. Other additional considerations include the alternative methods of selling, distribution, or advertising, the number and types of functions performed, the possible combination of markeuing inputs, and the dimensions of absolute marketing costs and revenue.

Marketing systems contain a wide variety of components, elements, and interrelationships that have infinite gradations. In addition, there is incomplete information concerning each element, so that marketing management always deals with systems under conditions of uncertainty. The complexity of the marketing decision problem is compounded by the large number of variables that are generated by the dynamic nature of the marketing process.

Large and complex marketing systems contain not only harmonious but also discordant or dysfunctional elements. For example, tension, strains, and conflict are intrinsic to marketing systems when one considers what is best for he wholesaler versus the retailer versus the manufacturer in a total system. The best course of action for the wholesaler may be the worth for the manufacturer.

Open Systems

Conceptually, marketing systems may be either open or closed; however, most marketing systems are open. An automatic vending machine is an example of a closed system. Known inputs (money) are put into the machine, and known outputs are obtained from it (provided the machine is working properly). Thus, the vending machine represents a highly, predictable, deterministic system.

Uncertainty plays an important role inmost marketing decisions. Results vary from those predicted because of changes in inputs and unpredicted variances in the states of the environment. Such systems are indeterminate and are frequently referred to as probabilistic systems. They present a more difficult planning and operating environment than does a closed system.

Intelligence Networks and System Adjustment

An important characteristic of a marketing system it the existence of complex intelligence networks. The intelligence network includes multiple feedback and forecast loops. Normally, marketing management feedback loops are thought of in terms of various marketing research, sales management, and distribution cost accounting activities, which provide management with information about events that have already occurred. Forecast loops may be viewed as providing future information derived through predictive processes, such as sales forecasting and simulations. The availability of pertinent past and future information is essential to system control and integration.

Marketing management has a prime responsibility for creative adaptation to change. Marketing systems must be constantly adjusted to changes in the marketplace. Information systems are necessary for recognition of new developments and management of marketing change. Despite the existence of complex intelligence networks, marketing systems do not automatically adjust to changing market conditions. The use of existing automatic control systems will not insure automatic adjustment of the marketing system. The present state of the art in information management has not produced a device similar to the servomechanism, which has widespread application in engineering.

Automatic control mechanisms cannot be instituted in most areas of marketing, although it is sometimes possible to set up an automatic control system for certain routine inventory decisions. Marketing activity is at a stage of development where human beings are involved in controlling the direction of company activity to a considerable extent.

Continuing advances in electronic data processing technology and in systems and procedures applications will improve marketing intelligence. Marketing managers will be provided with more timely, pertinent, dependable information on which to base decisions. Marketing activities generate huge quantities of data, from which essential information can probably be best assembled and communicated through computer processing. Improved control and more rapid adjustment of marketing systems should result from new and increased computer applications to marketing problems. For example, market simulation computer problems now provide strategic information that is not available through any other means.

Competition and Change

A characteristic of most marketing systems in free enterprise and mixed economies is that they are competitive. Each competitor faces opponents who constantly seek to promote their individual advantages. Competitors can be expected to react to offensive strategies with either a defensive strategy or a new offensive effort. Thus, marketing managers are faced with the problem of evaluating the probable effects of not only their own decisions but also their competitors' reactions. Maintenance of market position and growth of the firm require a willingness and ability to change.

The marketing system is characterized as a system constantly adjusting its elements and focus. The interaction of changing technology, research and development, shifting consumer attitudes and opinions, together with competition, necessitate continues system adjustment. The marketing manager must plan for change and accept it as an integral part of the systems approach to marketing.

REFERENCES

1. See Arthur D. Hall, "A Methodology for Systems Engineering," (Toronto, Canada: Van Nostrand, 1962), p. 60.
2. Stafford Beer, "What Has Cybernetics To Do With Operational Research?" *Operational Research Quarterly*, Vol. X, No. 1 (March, 1959), p. 3.
3. For a discussion of this classification, see Wroe Alderson, *Dynamic Marketing Behavior* (Homewood, III.: Richard D. Irwin, Inc., 1965), chap.1.
4. J.L. Henderson, *The Order of Nature* (Cambridge, Mass: Harvard University Press, 1917), p. 172.
5. Adapted from Herman E. Koenig, "Theory of Modeling Socio-Economic Systems," mimeographed paper. Department of electrical Engineering, Michigan State University, p. 12.
6. W.M.A. Brooker, "the Total Systems Myth," *Systems and Procedures*

Journal (July-August, 1965), p. 29.

7. Jay W. Forrester, "Industrial Dynamics," Harvard Business Review, Vol. XXXVI, No. 4 (July-August, 1958), p. 52.

8. O.R. Young, "A Survey of General Systems Theory," *General Systems*, Vol. IX (1984), pp. 6-62.

4

THE MARKETING SYSTEMS

Introduction

Marketing managers must be environmentalists, for external and internal environmental change is often the dominant factor in marketing decisions. The rate and magnitude of change and its effect on the firm in the form of innovations, flow of new products, and new competitive pressure are fundamental influences on marketing managers who are attempting to match customer needs and wants with corporate capabilities and resources.

The external environmental system surrounding the firm; it indicates the basic environmental forces that influence marketing strategy and performance. These forces are classified as: (1) scientific and technological, (2) life style and life space, (3) economic and political, and (4) ethical, legal, and social. Management's skill in meeting and adjusting to these forces is a significant determinant of the firm's profitability and growth. The articles in this chapter discuss the impact of these environmental forces on such important marketing variables as the consumer, corporate planning, and marketing strategy.

As technology and value systems change, new business problems and opportunities are created by a "society in motion." Consumption patterns, for example, are continually modified and altered by life style forces. These changing patterns are exemplified in the higher aspiration levels and goals of consumers.

Constantly evolving consumer attitudes toward products and services create a need for new marketing tactics. The study of life style forces contributes to the marketing manager's awareness and understanding of the complexity of consumer behaviour, and ultimately to more efficient marketing by the firm.

Technological change may be the major environmental force for many firms. We live in a period when 90 per cent of all the scientists in the world's history are alive, and the majority of man's store of scientific literature has been published in the last decade. Thus, it is not difficult to appreciate why marketing management must become increasingly aware of technological developments if they are to focus the firm's resources on the needs of to days dynamic markets. Environmental force interact, as indicated to create marketing problems and opportunities. For example, technology and changing life styles can interact to create a major force for change, as Marshall McLuhan has noted in his evaluation of the impact of television and other communications media on society. Developments in communications technology are shrinking distances and time scales, and the scope of marketing and market concepts must be adjusted accordingly.

Marketing problems should be solved and marketing opportunities developed in light of existing political, economic, and institutional forces. Consideration of these forces is contributing to a broader view of the firm's responsibility to society. Public policy decisions have significant effects on marketing decisions. Marketing decisions, in turn, influence public policy. Marketing managers and public policymakers can make a significant contribution to the process of constructive innovation and to society through the integration of private and public objectives. An effective marketing system is essential to economic growth, not only for a developing nation, but also for a mature economy.

Ethical considerations constitute another environmental force acting on the marketing decision maker. Because marketing is a logical focal pint for ethical evaluations of business, marketing managers should integrate ethical values and scientific marketing procedures. Present-day marketing cannot be understood without recognition of both domestic and international economic and political forces. The emergence of multinational enterprises is none development arising from and contributing to such forces. Competitive pressures in the American economy, together wit other environmental forces, create the necessity for a market orientation in which the consumer becomes the focal point of all corporate activity.

Formulation of a marketing strategy requires determination of an optimal customer-satisfactions mix. Marketing resources and procedures are combined with market segmentation factors and focused on customer needs and satisfactions. The degree of success in blending these elements into a workable strategy is determined by management's skills in planning and establishing corporate goals and in the coordinating of marketing management's systemic functions. These functions and their relationships are depicted. Achievement of the fir's goal and marketing objectives depends on customer response to its marketing mix.

Marketing Action and the External Environments

Life style is an important concept for marketers, because marketing is both a product and a determinant of life style. Life style facilitates the understanding, explanation and prediction of consumer behaviour. It also influences economic activity.

Life Style Concepts and Marketing

A general concept, referred to vaguely as "life style," is being used by behavioural scientists, especially sociologists. The precise nature and scope of the concept is not clear. However, in interviews about life style, several behavioural scientists revealed that they understood its general meaning and its significance for research purposes. They were also willing to discuss relevant life-style research projects and to recommend a body of literature that reflected a life-style orientation. They did not, however, define the concept specifically, and none of the recommended literature contained a definition.

The Life Style Concept

What is life style? Life style is a systems concept. It refers to the distinctive or characteristic mode of living, in its aggregative and broadest sense, of a whole society or segment thereof. It is concerned with those unique ingredients or qualities which describe the style of life of some culture or group, and distinguish it from others. It embodies the patterns that develop and emerge from the dynamics of living in a society.

Life style, therefore, is the result of such forces as culture, values, resources, symbols, license, and sanction. From one perspective, the aggregate of consumer purchases, and the manner in which they are consumed, reflect a society's life style.

Following this defining it is logical to speak of the American life style, our family life styles, consumer life styles, the life style of various social strata, and the life style of specific groups in different stages of the life cycle.

In marketing we have been particularly interested in consumer life styles in terms of the way people individualize, and identify themselves as members of various groups, and the resulting patterns of living. For example, we have gathered and analyzed data on consumer incomes, age groups, and expenditure patterns for decades. The goal is not one of assembling statistics for the sake of statistical information. Rather it is one of translating statistical findings about consumers into models of consumer life styles that will permit us to understand and predict various dimensions of consumer behaviour, particularly purchase behaviour.

A life style hierarchy may be charted consisting of:

Culture and Society

Group and Individual

expectations and Values

Life Style Pattern and Values

Purchase Decisions

Market reaction of Consumers

Life style, therefore, is major behavioural concept for understanding, explaining, and predicting consumer and business behaviour. It is a more generalized concept than existing concepts of consumer behaviour that have been advanced in marketing. Such topics as mobility, leisure, social class, life cycle, status, conformity, mass, and the family as a consuming unit are all part of the life-style fabric. As a result, life-style studies could foster the unification of findings and theories related to consumer behaviour. In fact, life style is a point of interdisciplinary convergence among marketing and such subject-matter areas as sociology, social and cultural anthropology, psychology, demography, and social psychology.

Economists and marketing people seem to have a different perspective on the value of life style concepts and findings. In most economic studies the life style of a society is usually assumed or ignored. It is part of the "state of the art" and "other things being equal," statements. (One striking exception is Veblen who developed such concepts as vicarious consumption and vicarious leisure.)

By contrast, in marketing, life-style of actors are viewed as among the most important forces influencing and shaping economic activity. They are the very focus of a major part of marketing. Foote, for instance, has suggested that in essence marketers are becoming taste counselors.[1] If this is the case, marketing and life style are surely intertwined.

Since ours is a materialistic, acquisitive, thing-minded, abundant economy, marketing becomes one of the cores for understanding life styles. Therefore, marketing is in a position to make significant contribution to a number of life-style oriented disciplines. Moreover, since our life style is being emulated in other parts of the world, such as Europe, Japan and Latin America, a better understanding of our life style may also enhance economic development theory.

Marketing and the Life Style of Abundance

When we think of abundance, we usually perceive of the physical capabilities and potentialities of a society. Abundance, however, is also a result of the culture itself since it stems partly from physical factors and partly from cultural forces. In large measure, our economic abundance results from certain institutions in our society which affect our pattern of living.

Potter maintains that advertising is the institution identified with abundance, particularly American abundance.[2] However, the institution that is brought into being by abundance without previous emphasis or existence in the same form is the institution of marketing. It is marketing expressed not only in advertising forms, but in such forms as the emphasis upon consumption in our society, marketing research, marketing planning, the marketing concept, new approaches to product development, credit, the management of innovation, the utilization of effective merchandising techniques, and the cultivation of mass markets; that is the institution of abundance.

Ours is a business-dominated society. Hence, business influences our life styles as profoundly as any other force. One of the unique characteristics of American business, however, is the distinctive approach it adopts to marketing. Marketing has reached its most mature form and has had its greatest impact on life styles in the American economy.

Other cultures have made significant contributions to business thought and practice in such areas as business law, ethics, accounting, finance, production systems, and organisation theory. By contrast, marketing progress to date is uniquely attributable to the American life style, and it is being studied and emulated in other parts of the world. Such institutions and techniques as self service, supermarkets, discount houses, marketing research, credit plans, and packaging are spreading part of the American life style in many parts of the world.

In a life-style sense, marketing is an institution of social control. It is an institution of social control in the same sense the school and the home are. It exerts an extensive influence on our life style which I maintain is for the betterment of our social and economic life. Moreover, since marketing is responsible to a very large extent for our standard of living it is impossible to understand our culture fully, and hence our life style, without some comprehension of marketing.

The impact of marketing on our patterns of living, particularly advertising, has not been ignored. Advertising has been criticized pointedly, Toynbee, for example, writes that if t ere demonstrated to be true "that personal consumption stimulated by advertising is essential for growth and full employment in an economy of abundance...it would also demonstrate to my mind that an economy of abundance is a spiritually unhealthy way of life, and that the sooner we reform it the better... The moral that I draw is that a way of life based on personal consumption, stimulated by advertising, needs change."[3] These are strong indictments of unfavorable marketing influences on our life style and are reinforced by the writings of such people s Warne, Galbraith, and Schlesinger.

When abundance prevails, however, the limitations and constraints upon business and other parts of our life style shift. Potter writes: "The most critical point in the functioning of society shifts from production to consumption...the culture must be reoriented to convert the producer's into a consumer's culture...and the society must be adjusted to a new set of drives and values of which consumption is paramount."[4] this becomes the challenge of marketing in altering life styles in an abundant economy. Marketing becomes an instrument for changing production-oriented value into consumption-oriented norms.

Marketing and Values

Our basic value system determines the nature and significance of various social institutions. These fundamental values, moreover, are not merely the result of the whims of marketers. It is true that we live in a sensate culture, one which stresses sensory enjoyment, materialism and utilitarianism.[5] Consumers desire and can own those items and symbols that are associated wit status, achievement, and accomplishment. Material values have become important. Marketing responds to, and reinforces, such values in our abundant culture, and in so doing appeals to the senses and emphasizes materialism.

The life-style question still to be answered, however, is one concerning the relative desirability of our life style with such emphases as contrasted with other life styles. Great materialistic stress and accomplishment is not inherently sinful and bad. Moral values are not vitiated as many critics seem to think by substantial material acquisitions. In reality the improvement of material situations can lead to a greater recognition of intrinsic values, the lifting of general tastes, the enhancement of a moral climate and the direction of more attention to the appreciation of art and esthetics.

This I would suggest is occurring today. It has also been the pattern of the past. In history great artistic and cultural advancements are at least accompanied, if not shaped, by periods of flourishing trade and commerce.

The next marketing frontier may well be an inner one—the market of the mind and the personal development of consumers.[6] Marketing in the future may be geared to filling the needs of this inner frontier. One of its roles may be that of encouraging increasing expenditures by consumers, of both dollars and time, to develop themselves intellectually, socially, and morally. This has already been accomplished to a limited degree: witness the increasing demand for classical records, good books, the attendance at symphony concerts, the purchase of good oil paintings through mail order catalogues, and the support for the arts in general. Social critics, while prone to point out the undesirable impact of marketing on our life styles, have neglected to indicate the progress and contributions that have been made.

Life Style and Consumer Expectations

Part of the American life style may be referred to as the American Dream. A big difference exists between the American Dream with its expectations and the dreams and expectations of other countries. The gap, however, is narrowing.

The American Dream as a life style concept includes a belief in equality of opportunity to obtain a good standard of living, to acquire status and success in a community through individual initiative, determination, sacrifice and skill. It involves the contradictory concept of equality for all and the rank and status orderings that result in the social ladders so characteristic of the functioning of our complex society. It requires the maintenance of an open society with opportunity for upward economic and social movement and the availability of education which is a root for social achievement, occupational advancement, and higher incomes on a widespread basis. These aspects of the Dream are reflected in our life style.

In general, American consumers, especially younger consumers, in living out the Dream exude optimism for the future. They feel sure that tomorrow will be better than today. American consumers believe that they can continue to expand their consumption and increase their relative amount of pleasure rather than merely limit desires. They feel sure they can continue increasing the are of purchasing power under their control.

One result of this optimistic outlook is that American consumers see virtue not so much in curbing desires, but rather in realizing oneself by acquiring the necessary goods and symbols. This optimistic life style has a historical root, for a Kraus has pointed out, unlike the European who only hoped that tomorrow would be no worse than today, Americans felt cheated if tomorrow were not better than today.[7] This orientation is supported and reflected in such marketing concepts. and techniques as programmed innovation and product development, installment credit, advertising, sales promotion and merchandising activities.

Life Style and Change

In our life style we do not accept institutions, techniques, and products as permanent. Our society contains a rich tradition of expecting and anticipating change. This anticipation results from a conscious belief that change are normal, useful, helpful, and good. We seem to accept what appears to be good today and anticipate that it will be superseded by items that are superior tomorrow. The rather trite expression "innovate or perish" has rich meaning for businesses trying to meet the demands of our pattern of life.

Such an attitude is one of the foundations of aggressive marketing. Girod has written that in our culture, "Innovation, change, mobility, and movement are permanent traits," and that, "In stressing the need for innovation, Americans are fighting for the maintenance of this aspect of their way of life for permanency of the one thing to which they are attached."[8]

By contract, some other cultures which are more restrictive in their anticipations do not expect, hope for, or plan for any great change in their environment. They strive to maintain the status quo. In these cultures which are resolute against the suggestion of new ideas, new products, and new processes, marketing tends to play but a minor role.

To date, technological changes have had the greatest effect on our life styles. Changing methods of marketing are, however, very significant. Consider the effect on our life style, and the life style of other cultures, of supermarkets, self-service, discount houses, shopping centers, automatic vending machines, credit plans, new products, packages, and new communications techniques. Such process and service innovations will have an even greater effect in the future.

Consumers, Consumption, and Life Style

In the scheme of our life style, because of a previous production orientation, the relative significance of consumers and consumption as economic determinants has been under-emphasized. The importance of maintaining physical production is, of course, widely recognized. Only limited reference, however, is made to the corresponding necessity of maintaining consumption. The critical nature of consumption in an abundant economy demands that consumption should not be considered as a happenstance activity. We must establish the necessary conditions for consumption to proceed on an adequate and orderly basis.

Until recently, even the relative significance of consumer investment in our economy was greatly under-emphasized. Business investment, which is certainly a most significant factor in influencing business conditions, received almost all the attention. Katona points out, however, that "growth and expansion of the American economy are dependent on consumer investment as well as business investment...business investment and consumer investment are equally important forces which either stimulate or retard the economy."[9]

What must also be recognized is the important fact that consumer investments are not merely the function of increased income. They stem from and reflect life styles.

A distorted picture has been presented of consumers and the purchase and consumption process. Consumers have been portrayed in much of the non-marketing literature as emotional, irrational, union formed beings, manipulated at will through marketing devices. It is held that conformity, followership, waste, ostentation, and meaningless style changes have been foisted upon consumers by marketers. Rokeach points out, however, that marketers have been using the wrong psychological theory. He emphasizes that the theory that consumers are irrational creatures who must be appealed to only on an emotional level is outmoded. Modern psychological theories view man as "not only a rationalizing creature but also a rational creature curious, exploratory and receptive to new ideas."[10]

Competition as Part of Our Life Style

Essentially, competition is directly related to and can be defined only in terms of the culture and nature of the environment that surrounds it. Competition has its fullest meaning in the marketing environment of a consumeristic economy rather than in a controlled, planned, or cooperative environment such as exists in many other countries.

In thinking about competition, however, we tend to be retrospective and do not relate it to current life styles. In interpreting laws and in our economic analysis we often cling to past or previous models of competition and competitive situations. For example, we often conceptualize competition in terms of an emerging industrial society rather than a maturing industrial society, in terms of price competition neglecting convenience and service competition, in terms of an economy of scarcity with relatively low consumer purchasing power rather than an economy of abundance with widespread discretionary purchasing power; in terms of manufacturers and distributors controlling and dominating the market place rather than an economy governed (or at least influenced to a large extent) by customer sovereignty: and in terms of intra-industry competition rather than inter-industry competition.

In particular, there is a misplaced emphasis, stemming from past economic models, on *price* as the key competitive weapon. This does not mean that price competition is no longer important in our mode of living. Certainly it is. It does mean, however, that ours is a competitive situation in which *price obscurity* and not price clarity seems to be the rule and in which other variables including convenience and service are very important.[11]

We seem to take competition for granted as one of the inherent aspects of our life style. J.M. Clark points out, however, that 'There can be no certainly that competition will remain vigorous in American business," and that "The necessary conditions are a fascinating subject for speculation." The necessary and sufficient condition for the existence of keen, vigorous competition, however, is clear. It is aggressive marketing. Changes in price, advertising, products, and channels of distribution tend to keep things stirred up and prevent competition from lapsing into routine passivity.[12]

Conclusion

To a large extend our marketing technology sets us apart from other cultures. It is a motivating force behind our competitive system and characterizes our life style. Marketing in the future must be recognized as a major institution in our way of life as well as a force that can contribute greatly to the influence of international life styles.

Yet analysts of our culture and life styles have virtually ignored marketing. It is often regarded as but a minor type of activity which is not important enough to be investigated. It has been neglected by psychologists, sociologists, social and cultural anthropologists, economists, and historians. It is treated as though it were a side issue in our economic activity, when in essence, it is one of the core or focal points.

Marketing is one of the longstanding institutions in our society. Is impact reverberates throughout our culture. It has shaped our life styles and has affected ever one of us significantly. The inextricable intertwinement of marketing and our life style was emphasized by a theologian who wrote, "The saintly cannot be separated from the market place for it is in the market place that man's future is being decided, they must be schooled in the arts of the market place as in the discipline of saintliness itself."[13]

REFERENCES

1. Nelson Foote, "he Anatomy of the Consumer," in Lincoln H. Clark, ed. *Consumer Behaviour, The Dynamics of Consumer Reaction*, New York University Press, pp. 21.24.
2. David M. Potter, People of Plenty, The University of Chicago Press, Chicago, 1954, p. 167.
3. Toynbee vs. Bernbach: As Advertising Morally Defensible?" *Yale Daily News*, Special Issue, 1963, p. 2.
4. Potter, op. cit., p. 173.
5. See Pitirim A. Sorokin, *The Crisis of Our Age*, New York, E.P. Dutton & Co., Inc., 1946, especially Chapter III.
6. For a discussion of this point see William Lazer & Eugene . Kelley, "Editorial Postscript," *Managerial Marketing: Perspectives & Viewpoints* (rev. ed.; Hotnewood, III.: Richard D. Irwin, Inc., 1963), p. 683.
7. See Michael Kraus, "The United States to 1865," The University of Michigan Press, Ann Harbor, Michigan, 1959.
8. Roger Girod, "Comment on Consumer Reaction to Innovation," In Lincoln H. Clark, ed. *Consumer Behavior, Research on Consumer Reactions*, Harper & Brothers, New York, 1958, p. 10.
9. George Katona, *Michigan Business Review*, July 161, pp. 17-20.
10. *New York Times*, November 7, 1963, p. 60, "Advertising: A Wrong Psychological Limb?"
11. See Eugene J. Kelley, "The Importance of Convenience in Consumer Purchasing," *Journal of Marketing*, July 1958. (Also

reprinted in this book, pp. 155-62).

12. J.M. Clark, "Competition: Static Models and Dynamic Aspects," *American Economic Review*, Vol. XLV, No. 2, May 1955, p. 462.

13. Louis Finkelstein in Conference On The American Character, *Bulletin, Center For The Study of Democratic Institutions*, October, 1861, p. 6.

5

COMMENTARY ON LIFE STYLE

Marketing in its broadest sense is the medium through which the material goods and culture of a society are transmitted to its members. As the style of living of members of a society—consumers—changes, the media of distribution and the products and services marketed must also change, or be replaced. All social institutions face the threat of obsolescence in a period of rapid change. Life style analysis can help marketing institutions both to minimize the risk of lagging behind cultural needs and to render more effective consumer services profitably.

Marketing's concern with the satisfaction of consumer needs explains why concepts, insights, or tools useful in understanding consumer satisfactions and behaviour should receive the thoughtful consideration of all marketing people....

The idea of product symbolism has been accepted for some time. Bt to think of a consumer life as a symbol, or as a family living a patterned way of life, living a family theme and image, opens several research possibilities for academic markers and marketing research practitioners. A manufacturer, for instance, could ask such questions as:

What are the firm's concepts about consumers and their ways of living?

What assumptions about consumer life styles underlie the advertising and marketing decisions made recently in the firm?

How do these assumptions check out with the realities of consumer life style patterns?

How can our concepts of consumer behaviour be sharpened through life style analysis?

Life Style Analysis reminds us that the consumer is indeed a complex person operating in a complex world. The approach forces an examination of the values and objectives of individuals under social settings in which consumers live. Perhaps one of the great values of life style analysis is that it raises certain questions about consumers and that it can bring information about such questions into marketing decision making.

Two of the greatest forces for change in the world today have life style dimensions. The movement to full citizenship of the American Negro is basically an ethical and social matter. But a movement which directly involves one tenth of our population is also bound to affect the style of living of the remainder. The revolution of rising expectations among people of the developing nations also represents life style movements just as basics to marketing men and to society as technological change. Less dramatic than these revolutionary social changes in the domestic and international markets are the changes in life styles of nearly all Americans. These changes will have a major impact on established institutions and firms, particularly those who do not develop and distribute consumer-satisfying products and services appropriate to changing technologies and modes of living... .

The gap between technology and modes of living seems to be widening. The problem is becoming both more complex and important because of the tremendous advances in technology which have taken place in recent years and the growing complexity of internal business operations within the fir. Management has a difficult task keeping up with technological changes and coping with complex internal problems resulting from the increasing scale of operation. When to this is added the rapid obsolescence of existing engineering management, and marketing knowledge, we can see why management's attention had been diverted from studying changes in the style of living of consumers toward the problems of changes in the style of management of business.

The marketing concept suggests that this may well be the wrong emphasis. Marketing minded firms might do well to begin with the life style needs of consumers and then attempt to integrate their technological research and development with the life style needs rather than the other way around....

The essence of marketing today is innovation, and life style analysis suggests many areas of profitable innovistic opportunity. In some cases, a study of consumption patterns in life style terms may suggest a substantial departure from traditional methods of marketing and doing business.

The implications are clear for a seller whose marketing thinking is geared to meeting the needs of fold life styles. Until quite recently many department stores resisted the new needs of a suburban population and continued to gear operations to their image of apartment dwelling consumers completely oriented to the central business district. American automobile manufacturers were quite slow to move to the compact car because they did not understand the new life style needs of an important market segment...

Life style translates into symbols so the symbolic meaning of products and services is something to be examined constantly by marketing people. Symbols are not merely status symbols, but symbols of a style of life. In an affluent society, the use to which people put products takes on more and more symbolic value. Professor Levy has earlier suggested the importance of symbols in the marketing world, particularly in regard to age, sex, and social class. As indicated earlier, marketers are not selling isolated products which can be viewed as symbols; they are selling, or consumers are buying, a style of life or pieces of a larger symbol.

The consumer can be perceived as following a system of

living, a family style. The job of marketing then becomes one of providing consumers with models of styles of living and the ingredients in which they, if they are so minded, can compose their own style of living, to reach their own inner frontiers as they satisfy material needs.

The question of applications of life style research is of interest. The prime value may be in the insights and perspectives the authors have stimulated. One of the greatest needs in marketing is for new concepts, and this concept seems most promising.

Life style analysis is valuable not only in terms of product development and adjustment, but once understood can be very effective in terms of the communications mix. Many marketing communication efforts are wasted because they emerge from an assessment of the style of living of consumers which misses reality.

How well do advertising and marketing men understand the nature of changing patterns of life style? Undoubtedly a great deal is known about consumers. Whether the right questions are asked is another subject in itself. Many advertisements seem to fly in the face of an elementary understanding of life style needs. The people in the ads are unreal, and the way in which they live is unreal. Browse through any consumer magazine and you can see the advertisers have a standard American life style in mind. They visualize, or seem to, their market as made up of beautiful and handsome people with several idealized children in an award-winning suburban setting. Happily such families are numerous in America today. But, consider how many people are not living this style of life or do not aspire to it. Where are the minority groups? Where are the poor people? Where are the senior citizens? Where are the non-Hollywood types? Where are the working wives? Where are the housewives who don't look as though they have two-car garages, all-electric kitchens, and white collar husbands?[1]

Life style approaches make it a little easier to take a new and longer special look at consumer behaviour. Focusing on the future to anticipate the nature of life style changes over a five or ten year period can bring a new dimension to marketing planning. The study of life style patterns can help sophisticated sellers see consumers as they exist today and are likely to look tomorrow. The danger of the kind of advertising mentioned is that it is self-deceptive to advertisers and marketers. We begin to believe it ourselves after a while and, therefore, to sell to consumers as we believe them to be.

Nelson Foote has suggested a question about how marketing fits into the changing life style of consumers. He asked whether we are correct in thinking that the consumer is an individual with constantly expanding needs, and that the job of marketing is just to move more goods and services, to build more shopping centers, stuff more homes, to keep turning out the goods which clog the closets, attics, and basements of America as well as its livingrooms.[2] As one speculation, is it possible that before the year 2000 the life style of consumers may not be as product oriented as it is today? It is possible, as Foote suggested, that we are seeing a pattern develop in which the consumer is devoting more of his attention to the satisfaction of wants that do not require consumption or production or distribution in the ordinary sense, but to inner satisfactions of a variety of kinds. He also pointed out that the customer of 2000 will experience as his first constraint not income, but time; as a second constraint, learning. Our very term "consumer' is a seller-defined term. People are not as likely to see themselves as consumers in the future, but as something else—perhaps as individuals creating their own style of living by using the services of business.

Several researchable questions suggested by David G. Moore are paraphrased below.[3] Such questions may be heard in consumer marketing research more often in the future.

1. What are the life problems and challenges perceived by various market segments in different life cycle stages as they relate to the product mission and opportunities of the firm?

2. How are these life problems and challenges likely to change over the next five to ten years for various market segments

as defined in both economic and social terms?

3. How do our present and programmed products and services help consumers deal with these challenges and problems? How can our products be improved in life style terms during the next five to ten year product-planning period?

4. How do customers use the products now available to them in their daily routines, as tools of activity, in their personal, social, and recreational lives, and as symbolic expressions of their desires and interests?

Such questions may challenge some marketers to do more work in defining consumer groups in life style and systems terms, establishing the goals of various market segments, and doing a more effective job of generating products and services which will help consumers deal with their most important problems. By moving in such direction, marketing can continue to fulfill its promise as an important social discipline concerned with the advancement of economic and social life.

A Universe-in-Motion Approach to Marketing

Significant marketing literature of the last half of the present century often relates marketing to relativity. This is because the tempo and inventive audacity of the times calls for a universe-in-motion approach to marketing. Nothing is static, all is ever changing and at a faster and faster pace. With the new marketing emphasis, for example, the term principles becomes old hat because it suggests the static; the term marketing concept is fashionable because it suggests progressiveness and change orientation.

The new approach suggests endlessness and fluidity. A business should be defined in terms of process rather than product (Theodore Levitt), a market is made up of shifting segments (Wendell Smith[4]), market is made up of shifting segments (Wendell Smith[5]) family buying units pass through life cycles (William H. Whyte, Jr.[6]).

The universe-in-motion characteristic abounds at this point in history for immensely significant reasons. The marketing manager must acutely be conscious of how the marketing environment relates to the pervading space time dimension. To cope with the fast-moving future, he must be change oriented for maximum effectiveness. This means he must ask if the way he looked at things in the past is appropriate for facing the future. Our present point in history especially, as this discussion will demonstrate, calls for a rethinking of fundamental concept. New concepts must be developed to assist in bridging today's yawning gap between what was and what is to be.

Creatively conceived concepts and theories must evolve before the world's vast new unknowns can be tackled if problems are to be faced in a methodical fashion.

Creatively conceived concepts and theories must evolve before the world's vast new unknowns can be tackled if problems are to be faced in a methodical fashion.

Concepts, theory, and philosophy serve practical purposes for they enhance efficiency of the thought process. They provide a needed reference framework so men, equipped with mental apparatus of limited scope, can assess new problems as they arise, make predictions, and pursue courses of action without constantly rethinking the premises involved.

The Three World Thought Eras Affecting Mankind

A look into history reveals a pattern of thought development that is most useful in formulating new thought frameworks for facing the future. Palenotologists estimate that man, at his present level of sophistication, has inhabited the earth for approximately 250,000 years. During this span of time, the intellectuality of man has been dominated by what may be called three major thought eras. Most of man's time on earth has been spent living during World Era I, or what could be called the Age of Ricualism, which extended back from Greece's Golden Age (450-300 B.C.) into the darkness of prehistory. During World Era I, man explained that things happened because the gods deemed them so. Man attempted to control and shape his destiny by appeasing the gods. The most sophisticated civilizations of the ritualistic ages, the ancient Egyptians in Africa, the Aztecs in Central America, and the peoples of India developed highly ritualistic societies – as characterized by pompous religious pyramids and temples, ceremonial burial methods, rigid caste stratifications of society, and stylized art forms.

The ritualistic World Era prevailed until the coming of Aristotle. This Greek genius, who lived from 384 to 321 B.C., ushered in World Era II, or what may be called the Age of Absolutism. Aristotle opened the flood gates of scientific inquiry for he taught the revolutionary idea of cause and effect. Artistotle introduced logic and divided intellectual inquiry into disciplines – mathematics, philosophy, astronomy, and so on. Thus, scholars could specialize in their pursuit of knowledge, record and store it so it could accumulate, be built upon, and passed n from generation to generation.

Aristotle's ideas prevailed until the coming of World Era III, or the Age of Relativity. Today's most sophisticated thinkers feel that absolutism is no longer appropriate to the times. Aristotle's ideas of logic and truth are now viewed as useful semantic means that make scientific inquiry and communication possible. Dr. Niels Bohr, Nobel Prize Winner and colleague of Einstein, writes:

Indeed, the general theory of relativity, by which Einstein in renouncing all ideas of absolute space and time gave our world picture a unity and harmony surpassing any previous dreams, offered an instructive lesson as regards the consistency and scope of plain language. The extension of physical experience in our days has...necessitated a radical revision of the foundation for the unambiguous use of our most elementary concepts, and has changed our attitude to the aim of physical science. Indeed, from our present standpoint physics is to be regarded not so much as the study of something a priori given, but rather as the development of methods for ordering and surveying human experience.[7]

Since the coming of Albert Einstein and his Law of Relativity, we know that nothing has a beginning or end. Allis flow, process, and rhythm. Truth, then is not fixed for eternity; it becomes, rather, the ability to predict accurately. Indeed, Heraclitus, a contemporary of Aristotle's, even at the dawn of the Age of Absolutism foresaw the Age of Relativity when he said, "You cannot step twice into the same river for fresh waters are ever flowing in upon you." What better advice can there be for the modern marketer than to suggest that he think in terms of the fresh aspects that flow into his environment, or in other words, that he make his decision only after looking into the future in terms of ever-changing variables?

Most of Man's Institutions are Obsolete

What bearing, then, has knowledge of the three World Eras on marketing? The marketing manager must know the cause of change so that he may manage it, capitalize on the opportunity it presents, and avoid the pitfalls it creates. Viewed in terms of modern man's 250,000 years on earth, the Age of Relativity is but a speck in time. It must be realized that the institutions man developed to cope with his environment have evolved from earlier ritualistic and absolutistic periods. It can be said that the institutions of family, religion, political organization, economic system, legal code and so on, are all under challenge because they are ritualistic-absolutistic and are to appropriate to the times of relativism. Today's review of its ancient tenets by the major Christian church, the state's questioning of the appropriateness of absolutistic legal procedures (divorce laws, penal codes, etc.), and the challenge of absolutistic forms of government, all provide examples of revolt or evolution away from our ritualistic-absolutistic heritage.

Not only man's institutions but also his art forms tie themselves to the three World Era concept. Dance, under the first World Era, was ritualistic, under the second absolutistic—dance steps were fixed—the minuet, waltz, etc. In the Age of Relativity, the dancer responds to whatever is felt to be appropriate to the immediate point in space and time—the Frug, Watusi, what-have-you. Art, under the Egyptians and Aztecs, was ritualistic-stylistic. A form of artistic representation was ritualistically fixed and was passed on from generation to generation. With the coming of Aristotle, art sought the truth—to paint and sculpt as realistically as possible—Rembrandt and Michelangelo represented the acme of this quest. Today, under relativity, art represents a feeling in space and time—surrealism, abstractionism and so on.

In the theater, the ancient Japanese No plays, largely incomprehensible tot eh modern Western mind, represent ritualistic theater. Shakespeare, and the Greek drama, where plays seek the truth about the nature of man and follow a true-to-life plot, demonstrate the peak of absolutistic theater. Today's non-plot Theater of the Absurd portends the theater art form of the Age of Relativity. In all areas of culture, the trio of the World Eras persists—in poetry it is the chant handed down from generation to generation (ritualism) versus the fixed verse forms of Shelley and Keats (absolutism) versus the free verse of today (relativism).

Relativity Relates to Marketing

Now how does this all relate to what is ahead in marketing? One example will alert the marketer as to how the switch from ritual-absolutism to relativity explains a present-day phenomenon directly related to marketing. The example is money. Under ritual-absolutism the ideal was to attain money that represented ritual symbolism and maintained absolute value. The history of economics offers endless examples of the search for the perfect money—embossed gold came closest to fulfilling the ideal. Today it can readily be seen that money in the ritual-absolutistic sense is obsolete. The flexibility of checks and the adaptability of credit cards both point to the development of monetary media designed to meet changing conditions in keeping wit the Age of Relativity. This convincing example of how the concept of money has altered to meet the needs of the three World Eras points up why it is important to think through the meaning of the coming of the Age of Relativity in terms of marketing. The concluding sections of this discussion analyze certain influences behind the times and relate them to marketing.

Ownership is An Anchronism[8]

Since the Garden of Eden, civilization's institutions and precepts have been base don two assumptions: that there is always a scarcity of material things, and that for the masses of people work is inevitable. But today these two assumptions are becoming less and less valid. For, as man comes to emphasize consumption, many of the precepts at the very base of his society must change. One key change lies in the attitudes he takes toward ownership. Such changes are already taking place. In the new world of technological affluence, the principle of ownership of material possessions by individuals is fast becoming an anachronism.

Through the ages, people placed value on ownership because there were not enough goods to go around. They were willing to accept ownership responsibilities to assure themselves of supplies of scarcities.

Reflect for a moment. How many people actually want to own an automobile, take home a "Handy six-bottle carrying case" of soft drinks, or have a drawer full of shirts they can call their own? In the final analysis, not many.

In reality, what they want is a car in the model of their choice, well maintained, kept in excellent mechanical condition, and at their disposal when they want it. Cars get bumps and scratches, brakes need relining, and all must be pampered into running and retaining their resale value. As for soft drinks, a person wants to have a cold drink in his hand when he wants it. "Handy" carrying cases imply returning bottles, lugging, and storing.

A man holds little affection for shirt as such. What he wants is a freshly laundered shirt with all buttons in place, in a weight and style to meet the seasonal and social situation he intends to face. Thus, people in a busy rapidly moving, affluent society increasingly realize that they are not interested in things per se, but rater in their use in a convenient and worry-free manner.

The Growing Importance of Time

The implication is clear. The affluent citizen of the next century will be oriented to buying time rather than product. He will take the myriad of sophisticated products at his disposal for granted. His chief concern will be to provide himself with free time in which he can conveniently use products that function to conserve time for leisure and pleasure. It is scarcity which creates value. Hence, as scarcity of product disappears, the scarcity of time ascends the value scale.

Since time grows more valuable as people grow in affluence, service expenditures increase proportionally as incomes rise. In the past, when domestic and service personnel were available, wealthy segments of society spent large proportions of income for service manpower (for housemaids, butlers, grooms, gardeners, game keepers, and so on). Thee helpers made time available so the wealthy could conveniently and pleasantly use their owned properties and possessions.

The affluent masses of today also seek to free time. However, because the personal service of domestics and service staffs is not available, the factory is expected to produce the wherewithal for freeing time. Throwaway goods; leasing communally owned facilities (where maintenance and servicing responsibilities are assumed at centrally located places that are staffed by experts); highly processed goods such as frozen foods, instant coffee, and the like (which provide a sort of built-in maid service)—all of these developments help to free time. In essence, citizens provide themselves with time by shedding themselves of ownership responsibilities.

Growth of Use Values Fosters Economic Stability

The realization by consumers that they prefer to spend their incomes for time-oriented use values rather than product-oriented asset ownership has enormous implications that are largely unrecognized. Use-value is realistic, for it relates to change; asset-ownership is absolutistic-ritualistic, for it is fixed and inflexible. An enticing aspect of the impending switch in consumer attitudes is that it holds a key to solving one of capitalism's basic problems, namely, the instability of employment.

Unemployment is a perpetual erosion which undermines the foundations of capitalism. During the first part f the twentieth century the idea emerged that modern capitalism's survival depended on its ability to provide continual production expansion. In the latter part of the twentieth century, two essential corollaries must be added to the goal of production expansion: (1) production must be steady, and (2) increased convenience must regularly be provided for products in order to facilitate their consumption. Most hopefully, the use-value doctrine can contribute to achieving these goals for stabilizing capitalistic economies. It is ironic that automation, which is roundly accused of causing unemployment, provides the affluence which will in the long run stabilize and expand employment.

Stabilization involves getting at one symptom of business cycles, namely, fluctuation in the rates at which individuals, industry, and government spend money. Fluctuations in spending reflect directly on production scheduling. Production must be steady, for this is the only means of assuring steady incomes for those who produce. Furthermore, efficiencies of automated production can only be fully realized when output is even and regular. Expansion or curtailment of automated manufacturing is so costly that its advantages are quickly lost when production fluctuates.

Stabilized production is also a necessary adjunct to introducing a still shorter workweek. The shorter workweek compounds problems in manufacturing and selling in feast-or-famine industries.

Elimination of fluctuations in spending requires that businessmen must increasingly apply their marketing ingenuity to secure regularly committed amounts from each individual's income.

The privilege of individuals doling out their incomes at any rate of speed or schedule they please will be a luxury which will have to be curtailed (not by fiat, but by persuasion) it we are to fully reap the material benefits of an automated world. The question is: Can we take advantage of the time-oriented use value to secure this effect?

If the goals of economic stability and full employment are to be achieved, marketing must be viewed as a social force. The public in general, and business leaders in particular, must better understand the place of marketing in the new society, for it is the force which will shape economic destiny by expanding and stabilizing consumption.

Methods for forcing consumption must be expanded and widely accepted as a permanent part of our social convention. The tempo of continuous consumption must be accelerated. Puritanical (absolutistic) attitudes (mothered all these centuries by scarcity) that view excessive consumption as immoral must be discarded. For example, the question of whether we basically need or even wish the goods that are produced is beside the point. Thinking in terms of conservation of replaceable resources will not solve the problems of the Age of Relativity.

The complexity of the problems involved in the social and economic adjustments which will be necessary to stabilize and increase the rate at which the private citizen spends his money staggers the imagination. However, the problems must and can be grasped with purposeful vigor. The largest roles in overcoming this Garguantuan challenge will be played by marketing men. In their hands lie the keys to selling merchandise so the family income is doled out in committed mounts, without interruption, and at accelerating rates. How this can be done is not so far-fetched as to evade the imagination.

Merchandising Non-Ownership

One of the more promising approaches to spending family income in committed amounts is either to lease merchandise or to sell it on a replenishment contract basis.

Many steps in the direction of contractual selling and leasing are already in evidence. As instances:

A large appliance manufacturer has announced the renting of home appliances to apartment-house owners. Not only will refrigerators, air conditioners, dishwashers, freezers, washers, and dryers be rented, but they will also be serviced and replaced by newer models.

Auto rental companies are already among the fastest expanding in our economy. One of the largest auto rental companies plans to extend a New York experiment with cars garaged directly n luxury apartments.

Department stores are promoting their own rental services. A leading store in Washington advertises availability of hundreds of items for rent, among them dishwashers, public address systems, lines, china, power tools, baby bassinettes, ad wheelchairs.

Even further steps are possible. Under a contract selling plan, which is a method for getting people used to leasing what they traditionally owned, automobile contracts could stipulate, for example, that a manufacturer will provide the family with a new automobile every three years. The amount paid each month would be fixed, and the all-important delivery date would be left to the discretion of the manufacturer.

Let us look at a hypothetical sales contract embellished with merchandising gimmicks. For customers entering into a contract for two, three, or four cars delivered at three-, six-, and nine-year intervals, the inducement might be a completed-contract "dividend" at the end of each three-year period which would make the next car 10% to 15% cheaper than one bought in the present manner.

Indeed, such savings dividends would be wholly practical since renewal sales costs would be small. Costs also would be reduced because the buyer under contract would be asked t indicate the model of car he wants perhaps six months in advance of delivery date. The buyer would choose his car by visiting a centrally located showroom where a complete range of the latest models would be displayed.

This method of advanced ordering would create the ideal situation manufacturers have dreamed about since the beginning of mass production, for it enables the manufacturer to plan production on a long-range basis. Certainly greater facility in planning ahead would lead to cost reductions that could be passed on to consumers. The promise-to-buy provision in the contract might be for a minimum of two cars with a right to cancel at the end of any three-year period, he penalty for canceling a contract being the loss of the 105 to 15% renewal dividend.

The selling format of the Book-of-the-Month Club, which has been widely adapted for selling things other than books, provides us with a precedent for this kind of selling. The method has already demonstrated that such contracts force sales, for it has sold many books that would otherwise never have been sold. It is also able to sell books the year round, doing much to compensate for Christmas and vacation sales peaks. Use of contractual selling means that competition would be as vigorous as ever, just as it is now among the book and record clubs.

Variations of contractual arrangements, such as those mentioned for automobiles, could be worked out for many lies of goods. For example, shoes could be provided at the rate of four pairs each year, for $5 per months; three suits a year, at $10 a month; and so on. This is actually not a far cry from the monthly payment of installment selling which is already well entrenched. Indeed, it seems that the British may have intuitively seen sales contracts and leasing coming, for they use the term "hire-purchase plan" when referring to selling on the installment basis.

Another convincing piece of evidence that contract selling is on the way is the extension by the automobile companies of service warranties, which have increased from 10,000 upto 100,000 miles in a short time. The warranty, in essence, is recognition that the customer prefers buying use-value and is not interested in ownership responsibility. Long warranties serve to stabilize the repair business, which illustrates in part how contractual selling serves to stabilize the economy as a whole. When a customer has a warranty, he brings his car in for repairs at the time the repair is needed. He is less inclined to postpone a repair for seasonal reasons, nor does he wait until the economic climate is right. Manufacturers benefit by being able to forecast parts and service requirements more accurately. Long-range planning can be entered into, the benefits of which can be passed along from supplier to supplier for end benefits to the company as a whole.

Two additional areas for expanding and stabilizing expenditures hold attractive potential. One area may be called throw-away consumption. This is the new world of disposable tableware such as plates, cups, tablecloths; single-use medical supplies such as needles, sheets, and dabbers; and portable and switchable building décor items such as curtains, partitions, and lighting fixtures. Expansion possibilities for disposables are unlimited. Consumer purchases of disposable items are continuous and regular and relate closely to use patterns.

The other area for steadying spending lies in the provision of centralized facilities for communal living. People living in apartment houses and suburban areas increasingly provide themselves with communal recreational and service facilities. Swimming pools and tennis courts, guest and reading rooms, and laundry and hobby shop facilities will increasingly be provided privately for smaller and smaller groups of people. Payment for such facilities becomes an adjunct to the monthly rent, a steady claim on income which is economically desirable.

By all these means, the increasing inclination of consumers to spend income for use-value instead of asset ownership can be capitalized on. This will help stabilize the economy to the extent that people thus are involved in long-term commitments that are paid for at regular intervals. In addition, people also tend to use up what they lease or contract more quickly since they do not take care of things as well. In this way, consumption also would be stepped up. Furthermore, requests for replacements for worn-out, obsolete, or otherwise unsuitable merchandise would be made as the need occurs; thus, the psychology of needing to make a decision to buy, that upsets economic stability, is bypassed.

The Marketer will be the Leader in a Silent Revolution

A review of emerging consumption-forcing methods which seek to expand and stabilize spending makes it clear that most of them (leasing, contract selling, consumption of disposables, communal facilities) do indeed relieve the citizen of property ownership responsibilities. Use-value rather than individual ownership implications dominate.

This silent revolution—which substitutes use-value for asset-ownership and raises the relative importance of time desirability over product desirability on the consumer's scale of values—has fantastically important implications for the business leader. Businessman must be counted on to provide the leadership which will gain the silent revolution victories in the marketplace.

The challenge to the businessman is two-dimensional. First, there is the social and economic dimension and the preservation and strengthening of capitalism. The business leader has to be aware of the magnitude of the silent revolution and understand the significance of how his role as the marketing leader and policy-maker is tied to production expansion and stabilized spending. Second, there is the business operational dimension. Here the silent revolution must be understood so that management decisions are geared to seizing the real business opportunities the Age of Relativity presents.

The change from the Ritualistic-Absolutistic to a Relativistic society implies that enlightened business leadership must increasingly understand and cater to the many needs and desires of a society in transition. Consumers, on the one hand, must be given to feel that their property-owning and conservation standards of the past are not violated. On the other hand, they must be made to feel comfortable about a future which will be more rootless, yet will have the modern advantages of providing free time for leisure, pleasure, convenience, mobility.

Correct business decisions will be made most frequently by leaders who understand these conflicting needs on the part of the consumer of the future. Furthermore, tomorrow's executives will have to be fast on their feet. Use-value emphasis will most certainly produce a market which reacts more quickly to various influences. An economy with no ownership can more rapidly embrace change and improvements, for there are no property franchises to disentrench or dispose of.

"Buy use, not ownership" is the rallying cry of the Age of Relativity. The idea is not so radical as a first-lush consideration of it may suggest. As has been shown, installment selling, extended warranties, and growth of leasing have already led us far along the road to divorcing the U.S. public from ownership. Further evidence that indicates trends leading to contractual spending are found in growth of prepaid medical service, payment of utilities and heating costs in 12 identical payments spread over a year, and rental of words of art by local art museums.

Provision for steady spending of the major portion of all incomes is the last link in the chain after mechanization, mass selling, mass credit, and well-being the world has ever seen. By promoting the goals of committed and expanded spending of incomes, the marketer's ingenguity can reduce business-cycle fluctuations and ensure prosperity. Theirs is the moral obligation to do this even if in the process they may e damned and misunderstood.

REFERENCES

1. For some examples indicating areas of advertising ignorance of the consumer, see Marya Mannes, "How Well Do advertisers Know the Consuming Public?" Proceedings, Thirty-Fifth Annual Boston Conference on Distribution, 1963, pp. 75-81.

2. Nelson N. Foote, "The Image of the Consumer in the Year 2000," Proceedings, Thirty-Fifth Annual Boston Conference on distribution, 1963, pp. 13-18.

3. See David G. Moore, "Life Styles in Bobile Suburbia," *Proceedings of the Spring Conference of the American Marketing Association,* 1963, pp. 151-63.

4. Theodore Levitt, "Marketing Myopia," *Harvard Business Review,* July-August, 1960.

5. Wendell R. Smith, "Product Differentiation and Market Segmentation as Alternative Marketing Strategies," *Journal of Marketing,* July, 1956, p. 3.

6. William. H Whyte, Jr., "Budgetism: Opiate of the Middle Class," Fortune, May, 1956.

7. From the essay *The Unity of Human Knowledge; in Essays 1958-*

1962 on Atomic Physics and Human Knowledge, by Niels Bohr, Inter-science Publishers, New York, 1963.

8. The concluding portions of this article, slightly altered, appeared in the *Harvard Business Review*, November-December, 1963.

6

MANAGEMENT OF TECHNOLOGICAL CHANGE

Since the marketing concept has become so well accepted, at least by marketing men, the role of marketing in managing technological change would seem to be fairly obvious. If satisfaction of consumer or customer needs is the dominating force in directing a business, it would appear that technological innovations should logically derive from the same source. I take no argument with this thesis expect to say that it doesn't always work that way. There are other forces that stimulate technological change and the process of innovation is more complex than simply finding a need and building a product, process, or service to satisfy it.

For one thing, the task of finding new consumer needs is somewhat difficult, because it is necessary to anticipate needs five or ten years hence. True technological innovation requires relatively long lead times; to produce anew product that will not satisfy requirements of future consumers is a useless exercise and a waste of money Fr another, the process of managing technological change or innovation requires consideration of a number of variables that are not always easy to isolate and measure. Finally, some of the strongest forces stimulating innovation are not consumer requirements, but business competition, making adequate use of available capital, and the sheer desire of the innovator to innovate.

Forces of Change in Business

Let's look at some of the forces in our business society that will tend to be dominating pressures on business leaders and that will affect the rate of future technological innovation.

The rapid growth of corporate funds is making it increasingly difficult for top management of companies to find good investment outlets. Internal sources of corporate funds have increased from about $11 billion in 1946 to around $38 billion in 1963. At the same time, external sources of funds – both long and short term – have hovered around the $10 billion maker. As a percentage of the total, internal sources have increased from about 50% to 61% or 62% today. The main reasons for this increase are the accrual of funds for tax and dividend payments; the buildup of cash flow, primarily because of growing depreciation allowances; and the adoption of better cash management techniques.

Retained cash flow of 120 corporations in a Stanford Research Institute sample of manufacturing corporations increased from $3.3 billion in 1947 to $13.2 billion in 1965. This is an increase of 400%. In spite of the present disharmonies in he money market with record high interest rates, the long term outlook is for growing generation of internal capital.

The result is that many companies in the United States today have idle cash or are getting a marginal return on part of their funds. Many a board room echoes with semi-hushed question, "What are we going to do with all that money?" For lurking in the shadows is the spectre of the government (federal, state, and local), which might feel the money could be put to better use to benefit society. Virtually half of the firms that come to Stanford Research Institute seeking research assistance in planning and corporate strategy are faced with the problem of new investment for idle funds.

Attempts to solve this growing problem will probably take many forms in the coming decade – all of which have implications for marketing men. The first of these is a growing channeling of funds toward overseas investment in the industrialized nations. Capital expenditures abroad have been advancing strongly since

1957. In spite of current efforts on the part of the United States and some foreign governments to retard additional U.S. investment abroad, the coming decade will see an increase in this kind of outlay. Most European nations do not have enough capital to finance their long term industrial development, ad the U.S. balance of payments problem may well be alleviated within the next three to four years. We will also see more investment in the underdeveloped nations and in Australia and Japan...

A second outlet for excess cash will be a diversification by many companies into financial operations. A number of companies that produce consumer products have set up captive finance companies. Others have established subsidiaries to finance dealers or other businesses. Although the among of capital that may be absorbed in this manner may not be great, the advantages of financial subsidiaries are substantial, and the number of captive finance companies will grow over the next ten years. Marketing men have an obvious stake in this sort of development. If anything, such activities will make product acquisition by the customer easier. Competition in financing terms is likely to grow, and, if you aren't now, you soon many be selling the payments—not the product.

A third use of corporate funds will probably have profound long term effects on the economy and marketing—more profound perhaps than any of the others. This is the channeling of more money into innovation—to research on products, processes, and services. Research Expenditures in the United States have been rising at stupendous rates since World War II, but a large percentage of the money spent has come from the federal government. Today, about 70% of the more than $20 billion spent on research and development in the United States is federal funds. But industry now has the wherewithal to finance research, some of which has been begging for funding.

This form of channeling funds will be aided by another phenomenon in the business society. Mounting cash flow and the need to find profitable investment opportunities for these funds have contributed to the growth of mergers, acquisitions, and diversification in U.S. industry. Over the next decade, however, antitrust considerations will make it increasingly difficult for large corporations and even some medium-sized ones to find suitable candidates for merge or acquisition....

Now this is somewhat of an old song. But this time the old song has a new verse—and even the harmonics are different. Enormous quantities of capital will be needed by industry for expansion, and that capital is available. Increasing shares of this capital will be used for research on new products, processes, and services, and for developing new markets. The markets are big and they are getting bigger. But the number of products to satiate the markets is even grater. The new products and services will satisfy old needs better than ever, and will awaken new needs that we didn't know existed. They will be more sophisticated, more utilitarian, and of greater value than their counterparts today.

The burgeoning availability of capital and the need for new outlets will create new opportunities and problems, for those associated with the marketing process. The need for technological innovation does not automatically imply that there will be wise investment in innovation. Indeed, one of the major false assumptions of our age is that change, by definition, is good. However, least there be some confusion about my attitude, I firmly believe in change—that I, change for the better. And the best way to achieve good technological change (or any other kind) is to manage it.

Managing Change

The fact that men seek to manage change is a unique characteristic of modern industrial life. Men are increasingly confident that they can shape their environment rather than be its creatures. This attitude has evolved gradually in Western society, but has been strikingly emphasized in the past few decades. That people who have lived for centuries in static societies have suddenly been caught up in a "revolution of rising expectations" is testimony to the validity of the concept. All men seek to grow, and growth is enhanced if the environment can be adapted to conditions that foster growth.

To foster growth, men plan. Men have always thought about the future. They have wished about it and daydreamed about it. Some have made attempts to shape it by planning about it. The new thing about planning is not that it exist, but that it is being done in a rigorous, formalized manner.

Planning is the process of thinking ahead and making a predetermination about a course of action. That business firms have begun to do this systematically, using standard procedures, has been occasioned by the growing size and complexity of business enterprise as well as by the increasing rapidly of changes in the business environment. Planning is an attempt to do more than respond to the environment. It is an effort to think ahead, to select a course of action, and to manage the environment so that events can be anticipated.

Managing Innovation

One of the key factors in the process of technological change is the management of innovation. Industrial firms must master the process of innovation rather than being buffeted by it, if they wish to grow and prosper. Mastering innovation does not imply resorting to instant invention—that is, just hiring a team of scientists, adding money, and hoping for automatic results, Innovation is more complex and comprehensive than that.

Genuine innovation covers much ore than technology. It includes innovation in production, finance, administration, marketing, and all other functions of business. Seeking technological innovation without considering improvement in the other elements of the enterprise is comparable to putting a modern jet engine in a DC-3 airframe.

Successful technological innovation occurs when it is considered in a broad context, embracing all of the environments in which the business firm operates. It isn't a question of whether to integrate science, technology, and marketing management, for it is done in some manner by some mechanism. The question is how to integrate these factors most efficiently to enhance the opportunities for technological and marketing success.

Knowledge of the Environments

To manage technological change, it is vital to have a knowledge of the environments—business, technological, political, and social. Every company has knowledge about itself. And, if the company is astute, it has reasonably accurate intelligence about the industry in which it operates. Knowledge of the company and its industry constitute partial knowledge of its environments. These particular environments are either friendly or hostile, and by knowing about them the company has some degree of control or response to changes within them. But equally important is the requirement for knowledge of what is occurring in the vast areas outside the company's immediate periphery. In large part, this wide environment is unknown, and in order to grow, innovate, and manage change, a business must convert its unknown environment to a known (and hopefully, friendly) one. If the environment is friendly, it presents an opportunity for innovation. If it is hostile, it presents a threat to the continued success of the enterprise, and some form of innovation is required to respond to the challenge...

Inputs to Innovation

Mateched against the need for a knowledge of the various environment is the need for an understanding of the inputs to innovation or certain criteria that must be examined and met if an innovation is to be successful. There are five major criteria: The needs of the market or user, the product concept, the state of the art, competition, and timing. I have not listed cost and price as criteria because they underlie and are the result of all of the others.

Genuine innovation stems from a requirement to satisfy the needs of people. Today, needs are not as obvious or as simple as they once were, and relatively complex goods and services are required to meet them. The prudent supplier of goods is faced with a prudent buyer; in addition, he is faced with a plethora of trends and countertrends, all of which augur an accelerating rate of change.

By identifying trends in the business, technological, political, and social environments, we can begin to get some idea of the needs of people. Some trends reinforce each other. Consider, for example, the trends of growing disposable income, increased leisure time, lengthened life spans, increasing educational attainment, growing job boredom among white collar workers, and an increasing "professionalization" among business people. This combination creates a receptive environment for products and services to fulfill a growing desire for education and recreation. In another instance, the growth of population, the increase in government activity, the expending size of businesses, the increasing complexity of business enterprise, and the inadequacy of data for decision-making indicate a need for improved communication and information systems. The real focus in this kind of trend analysis is to identify the needs of tomorrow's customers, not today's. Through observing the environmental trends and identifying where and how these trends reinforce each other, organizations can obtain some insight into the needs of users five and ten years hence.

The product concept is the set of ideas describing a product, process, or service that will meet a user or market need. The path we are following has a sign on it which says, "necessity is the mother of invention." Product concepts are usually developed from an analysis of user needs. If people could just say what they need, the problem would be simple; but, unfortunately, they usually don't know. The trick is to look at thinks in a different perspective so that imperfections in the present order of things can be identified. By doing this, new needs can be generated, and new product concepts can be identified to fulfill those needs.

Most often, product concepts will require determining whether the current state of the art is sufficiently advanced to fulfill their specifications. This can frequently be done with existing technology, but sometimes it calls for new and improved technology. Occasionally, it demands new scientific understanding. Such was the case in the development of the transistor. In his efforts to obtain a solid-state device that would amplify, Dr. Schocley obtained some unexpected results from his experiments.

These results demanded new theory. The new theory necessitated additional experiments to verify it. Additional unexpected results led to the junction transistor, which is the basis for the industry as we know it today. The results also led to a far better understanding of solid-state physics, the effects of which will be felt for many years.

The examination of the state of the art should not be limited to technology, but should ask questions concerning marketing and distribution, production, finance, manpower, administration—in other words, all of the major business functions.

Consideration of competitive conditions should embrace more than traditional competition for markets. Competition for funds, manpower, and physical resources, as well as competition with substitutes and governmental bodies, should be reviewed. It is important to analyze competition thoroughly within and among technologies as they apply to the projected innovation.

As marketing men readily recognize, timing is supremely important in the introduction of innovations. All four other criteria for a successful innovation may be favourable, but poor timing can ruin the entire under-taking. Timing may be too early as well as too late. Remember the Airflow Chrysler? The need was identified, the product concept of a streamlined automobile was sound, the state of the art was such that it could be built, and Chrysler was far ahead of the competition. But the timing was off. The auto was in advance of its time, was not readily accepted, and the innovation floundered, leaving a scar on that company that took years to overcome.

The Role of Marketing in Managing Innovation

Given all the environments that stimulate or impede innovation and the factors that must be considered in the innovative process, what then is the role of marketing in managing innovation?

To examine this role, let us array the various environments—business, technological, political, and social—in a matrix with the criteria for innovation. By examining the interfaces or squares and the kinds of problems involved in each, we can estimate the role of marketing in managing innovation. Figure 1 indicates the major and moderate roles that marketing plays in each instance.

It is important to note that marketing plays a role in all sectors of the matrix. It is not confined to an examination of the needs of the market or to a look at the social environment.

As shown in Figure 1, marketing's strongest roles are in establishing the needs of the market and in determining whether the product concept meets those needs. There are lesser but important inputs to be made in considering the state of the art, competition, and timing.

In establishing the needs of the market, marketing has the responsibility of examining consumer income trends, changes in the population mix, households, age and education patterns, and the like within the business environment. Similarly, it has a major role to play in identifying political encouragement or impedance within the political environment. The role of marketing in the social environment is obviously that of examining and detecting he values and attitudes of consumers or industrial users, the desire for product improvement, or such things as trends in consumer living patterns. It is primarily the function of R&D to examine the needs of the market in terms of the technological environment, but marketing has a moderate role to play in determining whether the market or users need and can accept an advanced and sophisticated technology or whether they require one that is less revolutionary.

In determining the product concept, marketing plays a strong role in the business, technological, and social environments. Does the product concept meet the needs of the user in terms of the business environment? Questions to be answered include those such as: Is the product concept oriented to the right population segments or age groups? Will rising personal income in European countries enable the product to be marketed there? Will inflation make a difference? Within the social environment, marketing is responsible for determining whether the product concept meets user requirements or falls short of the mark. In the technological areas, marketing's role is to help determine whether the technology makes the product overly complicated. It is also important that marketing ensure that the technology is being applied to the correct problem. In recent years, a host of companies rushed into the business of building teaching machines, only to fin that the problem was less one of designing an efficient device than of obtaining or developing the proper learning programs. The product concept must also be suitable to the political environment; it must be acceptable in terms of government regulations, and in line with government interests. In the beginning, the supersonic transport was primarily conceived to meet public and international policy needs rather than a burgeoning market. In California, vehicle exhaust control devices have had to meet specifications established by the state.

Examination of the state of the art is largely concerned with determining whether existing technology can do the job, or whether new technology needs to be developed. However, marketing has a moderate role to play in this instance by ensuring hat the proposed technology (existing or new) will produce a product that is priced right, will sell, and is economically feasible. Within the social environment, marketing then need to examine the state of their own art and determine whether present marketing methods are appropriate to marketing the innovation whether new ones need to be developed. For example, if service requirements for the product are unique or frequent, a new service organization may have to be established. It the product is high priced, replacement parts might be better supplied by air freight than by establishing complete stocks in regional warehouses.

In examining competition within the social environment, marketing's role need not be belabored. It is primarily is question of determining whether any competitor is offering a comparable product, and, if so, how the one contemplated can be superior. Marketing also has a major role to play in determining competition within the business environment, in terms of competition for salesmen, use of competitive advertising media, competition in financing, and the like. Marketing's role in assessing technological competition is fairly limited. Within the political environment the regulation of competition is an important factor for marketing to consider. As aerospace men can readily testify, marketing to government agencies is fraught with competition.

I have previously mentioned the importance of timing in terms of consumer acceptance of a new innovation. Less apparent perhaps is the role of marketing in ensuring

Introduction of a product at the correct time in the businesses cycle or in relation to other general business conditions. Marketing men may also lend a hand to those most concerned with technology n determining whether or not the product using the technology will be acceptable. For example, renovated sewerage for drinking water may be technologically (and even economically) feasible, but it may take a bit of consumer education before the timing is right.

Summary

The forces of change in business auger for a continuation and increase in the rate of technological innovation. The demand for new products to meet competition, utilize economic wealth, and satisfy the needs of increasingly independent and affluent consumers will channel more funs into technological innovation and create more technological change.

7

MARKETING AND PUBLIC POLICY

Character and Capacities of an Acceptable General Market System

A competitive general market system in a country such as the United States should not be conceptualized in terms of the economics of perfect competition. Hence, the market system is not synonomous with the functioning of the economy. Similarly, it is a mistake to conceptualize the market system or even market economy as synonomous with capitalism. Instead, the character and capacities of the market system must be conceptualized in terms of the historical background and drift, traditions, legal system and social and political goals and values of a nation or society.

If a nation or society wishes to (a) maintain a strong, widespread, and varied private enterprise base along with (b) free consumer-buyer choices among genuine alternatives and (c) "the rule of competition" in some acceptable degree, then the general market system must have the following interrelated capacities:

1. To respond to and aid the free choices of buyers at all levels, especially the choices of consumer-buyers, as mechanism of communication, coordination and

organization.

2. To respond to and interact with general and specific external environmental influences, forces and conditions (i.e., the system must be open ended).
3. To interact among the elements of the system internally, as an input-output system, including particularly the adjustment and shifting of resources from lesser advantaged uses to products, services, or geographical areas of greater advantage.
4. To allocate acceptably that portion of economic resources not allocated by government outside the market system.
5. To "regulate" in the sense of placing the participants under strong competitive compulsions for both (a) the efficient use of resources in production and in marketing, and (b) the effective fulfilment of the economic wants and desires of the members of the society....

Dual Impacts of Governmental Policies and Competition Upon Marketing and Growth Decisions of Private enterprise

We turn now to a brief interpretive appraisal of the dual impacts of competition under the market system and of governmental policies and regulations upon the basic market decisions and actions of private enterprise.

Commodity Versus Enterprise Competition

It is of high importance at this point to distinguish between two broad types of competition, which may be labeled "commodity" and "enterprise" competition. Always, of course, business enterprises are the producing ad marketing entities. But in the case of so-called "commodity competition," prices are definitely established for the enterprise's homogenous products by the impersonal supply and demand forces of the market. The problem of the enterprise is to collect, combine and use productive resources so efficiently as to a make profits and allow survival under the prices registered by a great macro-supply and demand cash register.

But in the case of "enterprise competition" the enterprise is in an environment, or creates one, in which profits and survival are not so clearly related to and determined by a simple price factor. The enterprise competes not only in the use of resources in production, but also in marketing and in "selling," In sense in this situation, the enterprise has its own micro-cash register which is still linked, however, with those of other enterprises (the macro-cash register) in a series of processes similar to those of modern computers linked together and also interacting with multiple remote control operators.

One test of the economic drift or trend of an economic society is the extent to which enterprises may be classified as under "commodity" or 'enterprise type" competition. Clearly, this distinction, too, has significance of or both the nature and functioning of the market system and appropriate public policy.

The discussion to follow is oriented primarily in terms of marketing decision s under the conditions of "enterprise competition" as now the more characteristic one in the United States.

Product Policies

On the whole product innovation, development and diversification are the bright spots under "enterprise competition" in the United States. The combined effects of governmental and private research and development and encouragement in a general environment of rapid scientific and technological change have given private enterprise an enormous dynamic, innovative thrust. On the whole, governmental policies and programmes are favourable, although there are unsettled issues concerning patent rights under governmentally sponsored Research and Development in some industries and of the new products in the food and drug industries.

Promotion Policies

In the main too, the environment in the United States is favorable to the use of personal and impersonal instruments and media for selling and promotion. This observation is of high importance because product innovation and development and promotion are parts of integrated processes. Time and again, we would not obtain the benefits of invention and innovation at all or as rapidly without effective promotion.

Product differentiation and promotion are supported by strong legal trademark and copyright protections. The chief thrust of public regulation is towards he protection of buyers, especially consumer-buyers, from deceit, falsehood and misrepresentation and to maintain conditions of fair competition among enterprises. On the whole, there is a relatively little public oversight of the use of personal selling, except through some local licensing. The focus of public regulation is upon impersonal selling or advertising in its various guises. Although such conjoined federal, state and local regulation often is onerous, the net effects on the whole usually are to support and channelize the competitive compulsion of the market system.

The chief burden of the public regulation of advertising is the protection of buyers, especially consumers, both with respect to quantity (weights and measures) and quality, and safety in use. Current public issues involve packaging (Hart Bill and consumer credit sales (Douglas Bill), and additional safeguards for uses in fields in which health and safety bulk high, as food and drugs and motor vehicles. In these and other instances, the problem of public regulation is to provide the requisite protection to buyers without encumbering business enterprises with unduly, detailed positive requirements.

Public issues in the field of promotion, important thought they may be, appear to be much less important and much more likely of reasonable mutual solution than in some other areas of business decision making. The chief ultimate risks could arise out of unnecessarily detailed prescriptions over business promotional behaviour. Promotional policies and practices should be, and for the most part are, amenable to reasonable regulation under a combination of private, individual and cooperative efforts and public oversight. In addition, legally recognized "puffing" provides some latitude and flexibility in sales promotion even in the face of stringent, positive regulations.

Pricing Policies and Practices

Public policy and regulation, like economic analysis, focuses strongly upon prices and pricing. Pricing is the holy of holies of antitrust enforcement with its per se prohibition of price conspiracies and strong suspicion of the conscious parallelism and price leadership of oligopolistic competition and of so-called administered pricing.

Public policies affecting pricing bring into shaper contrast the differences in market circumstances and compulsions affecting "commodity" and "enterprise" competition. On the one hand, there is a strong tendency to support prices artificially when under the pressures of sever commodity competition. On the other, aggressive price cutting by enterprises is under suspicion as "price chiselling' and unfair competition. There tends to be a contradictory interaction as between the efforts of antitrust to break down price conspiracies and to enhance competition and special federal and state legislation directed at the aggressive use of price cutting by individual enterprises.

Much of the controversy and issues in public regulation is centered about so-called "administered pricing," and what to do about it. In all of this there tends to be an inherent and basic contradition between public policies and regulations conceptualized in terms of traditional commodity competition and the complex, totality of business-getting variables, of which "net price" is but one, in enterprise competition.

The conflicts and issues affecting pricing are focused on three broad bodies of special regulation (1) under the Robinson-Patman Act addressed to price discrimination, (2) geographical, delivered pricing and (3) the resale price maintenance of branded goods. In not one of these broad, important areas of pricing has pubic policy achieved a reasonable, balanced relationship with the forces and compulsions of competition in and the market. In all three areas, there tends to be a general impact towards uniformity in pricing quite contrary to the accepted, *per se* prohibition of price agreements. The so-called "Fair Trade" laws allow manufacturers of trade-marked goods to impose uniform price structures upon the distributive trades when such action would be unlawful by their dealers themselves. Authorities agree that the net impacts of the enforcement of the Robinson-Patman Act probably have been towards restraint in pricing and a form of direct regulation country to the purposes of antitrust.

Oversight over geographical pricing has established clearly that organized, disciplined geographical, delivered price structures are unlawful in accordance with the general per se prohibition of price agreements. But there is a large zone of uncertainty and difference of attitudes and, in fact, a basic dilemma in enforcement under the conditions of "enterprise competition." On the one hand, systematic enforced delivered pricing structures on the part of business could subvert or even stifle the normal competitive forces and surplus and deficit adjustments of geographical competition in our great internal free trade market. On the other, simple enforcement solutions of the per se species on the part of enforcement agencies, if they run counter to basic market structural factors, could either be meaningless, or could produce a type of artificial, geographical price uniformity.

Marketing Organization of Individual Enterprises

Individual enterprises enjoy a great deal of freedom for choice among organizational alternatives to achieve marketing objectives, ranging from ownership and operation through vertical integration, through partial vertical integration, to a variety of exclusive and selective contractual and franshising arrangements. None of these forms of organization are illegal per se, but some are very nearly so. Thus, the acquisition of a competitor by a large firm raises legal risks so serious that most firms, especially large ones, would not wish to assume them. Thus, also, exclusive dealer or exclusive territorial arrangements are almost *per se* illegal for large enterprises with substantial volumes of sales. Similarly, franchise agreements by powerful manufacturers must be drawn carefully in relation to a strong presumption of unilateral control comparable to vertical integration with out all of its risks. The recent and current boom in franchise arrangements raises a host of unsettled legal issues.

In most public policy issues concerning organizational

arrangements, legal determination requires the analysis and appraisal of the special circumstances of the case in terms of the actual and probable effects upon competition. The spectrum of legal risks ranges from horizontal acquisition to vertical downstream integration, to vertical upstream integration, to the variety of exclusive and selective contractual arrangements. In general small and local enterprises enjoy grater elative freedom than large established national firms. The doctrine seems to be emerging that arrangements that would be restrictive of competition by large firms may aid and strengthen competition when employed by smaller firms.

Conclusion Concerning Conjoined Impacts of Governmental Polices and Competition upon Private Decision Making

It appears that private enterprise decisions and practices in product innovation, development and promotion, on the whole are in both a favourable competitive and public policy environment (with notable exceptions, of course). Public policy affecting pricing starts out bravely with its *per se* prohibition of price agreement but falters and to some extent reverses itself under the Robinson-Patman and Fair Trade Laws and shows signs of internal contradiction in geographical pricing. The broad drift of public policy affecting organizational arrangements seems increasingly to be oriented against restrictions and in opposition to growth in size, market share and vertical ownership and control, especially downstream and less so upstream. On the whole, the total net impact of governmental policies affecting private decision making, except in some strategic aspects of pricing, tend to support the internal competitive compulsions of the market system. The debits on the side of pricing may be more than offset by the credits on the side of product development and promotion.

Growth Policies and Market Structure

In recent years there has been an enormous interest in problems of economic growth in this country and even more so in the so-called undeveloped or underdeveloped countries. In the United States the discussion of National policies affecting economic growth have often been interlinked with discussions of the control of inflation and the maintenance of prices stability. Obviously, in a society with a private enterprise base, therefore, the impact of total national economic policies and of law and regulation upon growth incentives, opportunities and the patterns of growth of business firms is of highest importance. We shall omit from our discussion at this point national policies aimed at influencing aggregate demand by spending programmes, tax reduction and the like. Clearly, of course, these affect the marketing opportunities of private business. Insofar as such programmes can be timed appropriately and not used to weaken normal competitive forces, they can improve the environment of private opportunity. Our concern is more definitely with the effects of governmental regulations, including antitrust, upon incentives and policies for expansion and growth by individual firms.

First, in general, the intent of our national economic policies and regulations is not to inhibit growth of individual enterprises, except in one major respect to be discussed below, but to channelize it within the rules of the game. These rules comprise the great body of the law and regulations of unfair competition, abusive and predatory practices and behaviour and endeavours to monopolize. Such laws and regulations govern relations with competitors and suppliers and customers, i.e., all aspects of production and marketing.

Second, growth by internal expansion within the rules of the game is now looked upon much more favourably than growth by acquisitions and mergers, especially in antitrust enforcement. In general, it is believed that growth through ploughing back learnings and through gradual increase in the patronage of satisfied customers is more solid and substantial than by the acquisition of or merger wit established firms. From the point of view of antitrust it is held that growth internally expands investment and production and hence increases competition, while growth by merger and acquisition in some sense removes a competitor or a supplier or a customer from the market. In any event, there is no necessary increase in net investment or of production.

This view, when stated so simply, of course, disregards the

new investments and expansion of output that might be and often are made following a merger. Even so, it cannot be defined that if this same investment had been made in developing entirely new facilities in addition to the existing ones, total investment and hence competition could most likely be greater. Much will depend upon the special circumstances and especially upon the longer run trends, including the likelihood that the acquired firm would have failed in any event.

Third, the most critical issue affecting the growth of corporations in the United States is the trend of enforcement under the 1950 revision of Sec. 7 of the Clayton Act. As of the time of writing, the number and character of cases adjudicated and in process, and the weight of opinions by the Supreme Court of the United States in the small number of cases adjudicated, indicate that almost any merger or acquisition can be questioned, and a large proportion most likely negated. There is almost no large American corporation that does no now face one of the following problems: (1) the possibility that acquisitions made earlier may be questioned under "the backward bite" of antitrust, (2) whether to invest heavily in the improvement of recent acquisitions that might be questioned, or (3) whether to move forward with acquisitions under consideration.

American business now finds itself in a new environment so far as growth by mergers and acquisition is concerned. Under the present portents, it may well turn out that we have witnessed the last great merger movement n American history. If this be true, it could be of tremendous importance because many great American corporations were built to a considerable extent through the processes merger. To state this is not to deny the tremendous force of internal expansion separately or together with mergers.

Perhaps the most significant factor of all in terms of the maintenance and promotion of competition is that the entire force of action under Section 7 is to change market structure. But if existing and new firms are denied growth by acquisition, then powerful established corporations to some extent receive protection in growth through internal expansion. The successful, established forms whose growth by acquisition is most likely to be questioned are also the firms best equipped in terms of resources for growth through building new facilities. It would seem almost inevitable, therefore, that strong enforcement under revised Section 7 would at some stage involve an increasing interest in Big Cases under Section 2 of the Scherman Act. In other words, bigness and giantism, and concentration of market and economic power, would come to the front in antitrust policy both with respect to growth by internal expansion and growth by acquisition.

Very likely, the issues and drift on this score will be clarified somewhat when further cases involving conglomerate acquisitions are adjudicated, for these, in a very direct sense, focus upon *Bigness, per se,* or economic concentration as opposed to market concentration. But the cases adjudicated or now moving forward to the Supreme Court most likely will touch only upon peripheral issues. The determination of public policy on this issue probably will be in the political arena and not through the application of economic and marketing analysis in antitrust cases. Hopefully economics and marketing will not be disregarded entirely, however, in the political moves. The character of the testimony at recent hearings is an optimistic omen.

In public policy it was widely believed (with some dissident views) that investment diversification and growth by conglomerate acquisitions were relatively acceptable in contrast with horizontal and vertical integration and acquisitions. Horizontal expansion, especially by acquisitions, reduced competition on the same level. Vertical expansion, and especially acquisition, reduced competition presumably by removing or weakening a supplier or customer. But conglomerate diversification, broadly conceived, was held to increase competition by the entrance of established firms into new areas. In such moves, broad, inter-industry forces of competition could be promoted and presumably competition increased. But in recent years, a view has been arising that broad nonfunctional diversification, especially by the acquisition of established firms, is one of the greatest threats to competition through the exercise of "conglomerate power," allegedly a new, insidious type of monopoly power. As of new, it is impossible to reconcile these two views either in economic and managerial theory or in law and regulation. Again, we are forced to revert to the legal processes of case by case analysis and determination. Undoubtedly, conglomerate diversification at times strengthens the competitive compulsions of the market systems, and sometimes such overlapping of large corporations may be the only feasible means of doing so. Undoubtedly, too, the reverse does, or could occur, especially then large, powerful firms enter areas occupied by small local and regional enterprises. Undoubtedly, too, in public policy, some bounds must be provided to protect the market system from large indigestible globs that could become almost global in competitive outreach.

Very likely, too, in many situations, the character of the use of whatever "conglomerate power' may have been achieved, could be subject to control under either (1) Section 5 of the Federal Trade Commission Act governing unfair methods and practices of or (2) Sec. 1 of the Sherman Act governing the restraint of trade, without structural change. In this manner, the enhanced competitive impacts might be preserved but within the rules of the competitive game. Both persons and business enterprises can be expected to show restraint in the exercise of abilities and capacities. To made the mere possession of power to act the basis of action pushes regulation towards structural adjustments intended to enhance the impersonal compulsions of the market system. Whether this makes sense depends upon the actual and potential market structural and behavioural circumstances of each situation and cannot be answered in general terms.

Above all, it is a mistake to assume that the character and effectiveness of competition bear a simple, direct relationship to the number of competitors alone. Consequently, it could be a grievous error to take action based upon the mere presence of ability to act when (1) market structure adjustments would not in fact negate such power and (2) the beneficial aspects of enhanced competition could be preserved without abuse...

Appraisal in Terms of the Required Capacities of an Acceptable Market System

We are in a position now to generalize concerning the extent to which the general market system in the United States is able to exercise the five types of capacities suggested as essential for the maintenance of an acceptable, viable market system.

1. Response to and facilitation of buyer choices, especially of consumer buyers; In the main, the conclusion here is favourable, although many, including some top professional economists, will disagree. There is a widespread view that consumer sovereignty is a wasting, perhaps already wasted asset—that consumer choices are determined largely by a conjoined group behaviourism and Madison Avenue. No one, of course, is able to prove or disprove a generalization so sweeping and so subjective, and running so counter to the marketing experience of even the most powerful corporations. It would seem much more sensible for purposes of public policy in a democracy to accept the fact of consumer choice among genuine alternatives as given and then to continue to try to guarantee that the choices can be made from among genuine, honest, competitive alternates. The same conclusion would seem even more reasonable and easier to enforce at the other levels of buying choice The lack of opportunity for choice among independent alternatives might well be a major criterion in the selection of antitrust cases. Such opportunity, for choice, if at all possible, should be available at all levels and for all offerings in the market system.

2. Interaction to external environmental influences: Out market system is not a mechanical closed system but is open-ended and is responding to innumerable external pressures and influences including governmental regulations and intervention. There is not guarantee, however, that the net results of the interventions are beneficial in terms of maintaining a viable effective market system adequate for a society wit a private enterprise base. It would be an enormous contribution to make an objective considered estimate of the net effects and the general drift and tendencies.

3. Internal Interaction within the system: The interactions within the market system are focused most sharply on product (Out Put) markets instead of at the level of factor inputs.

Increasingly, the prices of factor inputs are being removed from determination by the market system or placed under the shared rule of governmental regulations and the market. This observation applies for example to labour, energy, freight, some raw materials, some services, and some communication inputs which are outside the market bargain, more or less. The Robinson-Patman Act tends also to place restraints over the input price level. A consequence of the to accentuate rendencies towards upstream vertical integration.

So far as the shifting of resources within the system from lesser continuing processes of innovative and of imitative competition. On the whole, the American marketing system displays enormous internal vitality in terms of the innovative, adaptive and imitative use of resources in "enterprise competition." When this does to occur, because of barriers to entry or agreement among competitors, then antitrust authorities should be interested and take the appropriate steps. The largest such areas in terms of economic analysis, of course, is allegedly the short term or long term strength of market position engendered by he successful product differentiation and brand promotion as noted earlier.

In this area, however, public policy must tread softly and deftly, because much of the high strategy and dynamism of American enterprise competition is found here, and must be so in the presence of a strong anticartel policy, let alone the magnitude of the potential gains of success in our rich national market amplified by multi-national opportunities. Furthermore, opportunity for differential gain along these lines must be held out to enterprises, in order to encourage and support the cots and risks of product innovation and development.

4. Ability to act as an allocating medium for resources not allocated by government outside the market system: To some extent, the allocating responsibility was discussed in the preceding section in terms of the internal interactions of the system. It remains to be noted, however, that in all societies, governments talks some direct responsibility for the allocation of much or all of the land, raw material and capital resources. In some underdeveloped countries the allocations of the market system

are either not trusted or are considered too slow for the purposes of economic development, and, in communist and socialist societies, the primary means of control under the Central Plan is through the allocation of basic resources.

But evening the United States, a large portion of resources allocation is outside the market system, through public ownership and employment, the public services, defense and military programmes, and tax collections and disbursements. It would be enormously help to have a solid estimate of the extent to which resource allocation occurs through the market mechanism in the United States, or is under a planned sharing of governmental regulation and the market.

In this connection there is a well publicized view that the market can or should have a decreasing role in a society of abundance, as in the Untied States. N other words, we should look forward to a broad expansion of the public services outside and in lieu of the market system. This view reflects to some extent (1) the belief that consumer sovereignty through the market has wasted away and (2) a higher degree of confidence in voting through the ballot box than through cash registers.

5. To regulate; i.e., to enforce the discipline of the "rule of competition": In the United States, the "rule of competition" is relief upon chiefly in the final, manufactured product markets and in the distributive trades. Insofar as market discipline has been removed from factor-input markets, its remaining impact is chiefly towards the efficient use of resources in production and in marketing in final product markets and in the effective fulfillment of given buyer choices or in market innovation. Obviously, this is a large important and strategic responsibility for the market system, especially because it is the medium for serving and influencing the ultimate consumers. This is also the accepted area of active antitrust enforcement, although recent indications suggest that antitrust, under new interpretations of areas of primary jurisdiction, may tend to become more effective in some of the factor-input markets than has been assumed traditionally, unless restrained by new specially legislation. It is in this area, too, that the chips as they fall, indicate the type

of society or position on the spectrum between a full command society or a full market society. And finally, it is here and in the trend of the allocation of basic resources, including capital resources, that the broad economic, political drift of a society can bet be observed.

8

ETHICS AND SCIENCE IN MARKETING

Ethical considerations are a dynamic environmental force influencing marketing decisions. Marketing is a logical focal point for ethical evaluations of business. Cultural evolution is the dynamic determinant of ethical attitudes toward management methods and objectives. Marketing managers must integrate current ethical values and scientific marketing approaches. To be successful, a firm's view of the societal responsibilities of marketing must equate with those currently held by society.

The challenge, as I see it, is that we have to be as dynamic, imaginative and research-minded in the ethical field as we have been in the scientific and materialistic fields. We must accept this new world as a new opportunity for being ethical. The case is far from hopeless.[1]

Research methodology and decisions in marketing are influenced by the interacting cultural approaches of the "manager," the "scientist," and the "humanist." These approaches are considered in this excerpt as they relate to ethics and science in marketing and to the social functions of marketing. The purpose of this excerpt is to raise some questions about the philosophical dimension of ethics as it relates to marketing. This is a relatively new area of marketing inquiry. The thoughts presented a designed to stimulate independent and intelligent thought about the ethical issues inherent in the practice of marketing.

In this excerpt, some marketing questions with ethical dimensions are identified, and the various factors involved in these questions are defined. The questions focus on the moral responsibilities of marketing decision makers. The social functions of marketing, including survival, profit-making, and social responsibility, are discussed, and the ethical stages of a discipline are indicated. Meta-marketing is presented as the vehicle by which marketing science and social responsibility can be integrated in meeting the challenges of these scientific revolution.

Some Marketing Ethics Questions

Some marketing questions with ethical dimensions include the following:

1. Are marketing scientists and individual contributors to marketing morally responsible for the marketing decisions to which they contribute their talents?

   This is not a new issue in business. For instance, in marketing the question of moral responsibility has arisen to confront advertising executive. Are executives in advertising agencies "morally responsible for the advertising they create," and "are media executives morally responsible for the advertising contents the media carry?"[2] a common position of advertising people in the face of such questions traditionally has been that the advertising agency is a technical service group with the job of creating and placing advertisements. Responsibility belongs with the client according to this view. Whether an agency is or is not morally responsible for client's claims or is or is not acting simply as a technician is a question being discussed n advertising today.

2. As an example, does the marketing scientist concerned with developing media allocation models have any responsibility for the messages carried in those media? Or is he only concerned with the techniques involved, not

with the messages sent to sell products of which he might not personally approve—cigarettes, liquor, or anything else?

3. Is a marketing scientist concerned with the ethics of persuading people to do something which might not be in their long-term interest? What are the responsibilities, ethically, of the motivation researcher and the manager who uses this findings? The ultimate objective of much research in marketing is to influence or manipulate purchase behaviour through probing into the consciousness of individual consumers. The question of the use to which the work of marketing scientists and individual contributors to marketing is put is a difficult one. Scientists in other fields have faced it. One conclusion of interest is that:

   It is inevitable that in the long run researchers as a group will have to be concerned with the applications of their work, in the same way that atomic scientists formed a federation so that as citizens they would have a voice in determining the utilization of what they had developed as technicians.[3]

4. Is the marketing scientist concerned with the ethical problems involved in programmes of planned product obsolescence. Many product programmes can be seen as efforts to make a product obsolete before it is completely worn out. Many projects in which marketing science studies are undertaken are done with the direct objective of rendering present products obsolete even though a measure of utility remains.

5. Is the marketing scientist concerned with any aspect of marketing other than the efficient movement of goods on a profitable basis? Does a marketing scientist have responsibility for developing standards for measuring contributions other than efficiency—perhaps by contributing to the development of "ethical science?"

6. There is some evidence that profits are taking on a subsidiary role in many business problems. Questions of economic

> and social stability, public relations, and a fear of government intervention have proved strong influences ion executive decisions in the past. These factors have modified the traditional view of the profit maximization objective to the extent that profit maximization rules provide limited guidance for business executives. Are there ethical implications of significance to marketing science in the development of the "corporate conscience" and the social responsibility view of business? There is a danger of becoming concerned for the sake of ethics alone. It has been suggested that an attitude of this kind can prove harmful and event undermine that enterprise system. Levitt has said, "In the end business has two responsibilities – to obey the canons of everyday face-to-face civility, (honesty, good faith and so on), and to seek material gain and to seize profit. Anything beyond this gets very complicated."[4]

Such questions can be answered on two levels. One is the level of facts. This is the area in which scientists deal or at least prefer to deal. Another is the ethical level. This level requires that standards for approval or disapproval be used.

Disagreements about the place of ethical issues in business sometimes reflect the fact that the conception and definition of ethics is often a highly personal matter. A set of definitions is offered here in the hope that it might facilitate discussion and further exploration of the questions raised in this chapter.

Definitions

Marketing

Marketing can be perceived as a field of management practice, as a social discipline, or as a developing science. As a field of business practice, marketing consists of the activities involved in the generation of markets and customers and in the development and distribution of customer-satisfying goods and services. As a socio-management activity, marketing includes all the tasks involved in the development and delivery of a flow of goods and services from production to consumption. As a social discipline, marketing is the study of the economic and social instrumentality through which a standard of living is delivered to consumers.

Marketing Science

Marketing science is the application of scientific method to marketing problems. One aspect of this science is the use of quantitative approaches to problem solving and decision making. The computer is one important tool of management science; more important is the scientific approach, which involves the use of reliable research methods to unearth valid marketing knowledge and the se of such knowledge in order to better attain marketing objectives. The task of the marketing scientist is to provide decision makers who have to responsibility of committing corporate resources with the scientific and technical input required to reduce or eliminate the areas of uncertainty in marketing problem solving.

Ethics

Ethics as used in this chapter refers to the philosophy of moral values or moral norms, that is, normative ethics. As used here, ethics does not belong to empirical science, but to a division of philosophy—the study and philosophy of human conduct with emphasis on the determination of right and wrong. By definition, it is concerned with good and evil, what is right and what is wrong, that should be, rater than what exists. As White stated, "The purpose of philosophical, or normative ethics is to take norms for human action or judgments about moral values."[5]

Moral Values

Moral values refer to the degree of conformity to right conduct. This involves questions of the sense of good, the true and right. History is replete with examples of men being actuated by a sense of good, true and right procedures to accomplish dubious or even satanic ends. Ethics refers to the rules of human behaviour considered right and proper by a society at a specified time. Moral becomes a descriptive adjective denoting a study of standard ethical behaviour.

Marketing Ethics

Marketing ethics is the area of marketing study and thought concerned with defining norms for judgments about the moral consequences of marketing actions. In practice, a marketing ethics is concerned with standards of adequate behaviour in terms of marketing policies and practices within legal and social constraints at a point in time. The concern of the theorist is with what is acceptable behaivour in terms of right and wrong in a culture at a point in time so that decision making can be more successful.

Ethics are not linked to any narrow part of life. It can be argued that there are "marketing ethics," that there may or may not be any "business ethics," and ethics are only a matter for individuals concerned with marketing or any other activity. Thus it is held there are no marketing ethics, medical ethics, or legal ethics, and ethics are considered as being concerned with all rational behaviour. Accordingly, criticisms of marketing activity are really criticisms of the level of ethics of a business system or of society. The criticism of marketing comes about, in this view, primarily because marketing is by nature more visible and conspicuous than other areas of business practice. The point of view of this chapter is that for analytical purposes it is at times useful to think of level of ethics in business and marketing as it exists at a point in decision time and place.

Meta-marketing

Meta-marketing (beyond marketing) as in metaphysics, meta-psychology, or in other disciplines, is used to designate a new, although related, discipline which deals critically with marketing as a discipline. All concerned with marketing can contribute to what may be this promising direction. Marketing is a discipline offering multiple opportunities for speculations on the inter-relationships of mental and physical processes to supplement the facts and empirical regularities of marketing science. Kane, in discussing the need for new approaches to planning methodology in national security planning, suggested the term "meta-planning" to seek to bring in the whole of experience and of the human personality to bear on planning.[6] The concern of meta-marketing is similar—to bring the whole of scientific, social, ethical, and managerial experience to bear on marketing.

The fact that disagreement exists about these terms reflects the fact that marketing is a field of study and a business activity with significant economic, social, and administrative dimensions. It is not surprising that an economist, mathematician, sociologist, or a manager would tend to define terms differently and that different approaches to definitions, and to research, produce different results. As Bartels said:

> Research findings are dependent not only upon the hypotheses, data, methodology, etc. Which comprise scientific research practice, but also upon subjective factors such as the researcher's area and intensity of interest, economic opportunism, social affiliations, personality, background, concepts and the like.[7]

An example is that some scientists are reluctant to raise ethical questions which involve moral judgments because such considerations do not advance the body of the science with which they are concerned. However, the interdisciplinary approach to marketing is providing to be of sufficient value so that some students are willing to explore the possible contributions of hybrid disciplines such as marketing ethics. Marketing science itself is essentially a "multisexual" discipline, to use a term from Boulding,[8] and a natural area of convergence for the interdisciplinary approach to business administration.

One indication that marketing is a natural focal point of ethical problems and considerations in business is that much government regulation is designed to govern marketing activities. Presumably, some regulation developed because of the feeling that businessmen were failing to regulate themselves according to the proper ethical standards. There is continuing dialogue between business and government on the question of regulation of business. The legal conflicts can be settled by legislation and the courts. The conflict discussed here between ethical concepts and marketing practice is philosophical. It exists because philosophers concerned with ethical issues are concerned with an ideal in which absolute ethical values and concepts are superimposed on the culture according to the highest moral values. But the standards of ethical behaviour in business which influence the area sin which management scientists operate are taken from the prevailing culture of the time. The standards may be far from the philosophic ideal. So, by definition, ethics is a subject which is not related primarily to business practices but rather to the promise and potential of a higher climate. Discussions of marketing issues with ethical dimensions can help to develop an appreciation of the relations between existing business practices and ethical concepts and standards.

While marketing scientists can abstract ethical and moral decisions from many problems, and students of marketing ethics can choose not to communicate with management scientists, management must face the task of integration. Management decision making inevitably involves the balancing of ethical and moral issues with scientific approaches. A manager rarely has to content with a problem which is exclusively a marketing science or a marketing ethics problem anymore than he has to contend with problems which are exclusively economic in nature. He deals routinely with complex, multidisciplinary problems.

One academic viewpoint is that problems of ethics and morality in business need not be discussed in any formed way in the business schools. (This attitude may be one reason why there are relatively few business ethics courses). Those holding this view, who think ethical questions should be discussed at all, feel that each teacher should handle ethical problems of business in his own course, just as each businessman should handle such problems in his own firm. Some marketing practitioners have also expressed doubt that fields called "Marketing Science" or "Marketing Theory" can be identified. Others accept the existence of these fields but see them as unrelated. Probably most readers of this chapter are willing to grant the existence of an area called marketing science. Perhaps not so many would be as tolerant of marketing ethics.

Managers are not usually concerned with whether they are "marketing scientists" or "ethical scientists." Their position is they are practicing executives attempting to manage the efforts of an organization to accomplish corporate objectives. Even though staff advice inside the business tends to come from men committed to one or another basic position, the manager does not normally expect the marketing scientist to integrate ethical considerations in the body of his science. Managers have long accepted the notion of division of labour, managers are prepared to integrate where their specialized staff and professional personnel are unwilling or unable to integrate. However, managers are usually pleased to find technicians who have the ability to do relational thinking. This ability is one measure of the person's ability to change roles from marketing scientist or social marketer to marketing management.

It may be that the survival of the enterprise system depends on the manager's ability to integrate the contributions of the scientist and of the ethical scientist or social philosopher. Ina university the marketing teacher might well have to consider the extent to which he should attempt the integration of the sometimes polarized forces of quantifiable goals and moral values.

The integrating task of management is no easier than the task of the social historian, political scientist, or economist who attempts to bridge cultures. One reason the integration problem for managers is complex, is that management theory and practice are in a transitional stage, and the manager is confronted with several diverse approaches to the problem of integrating ethical and science...

Social Functions of Marketing

Ethical issues are necessarily involved in any discussion of the social functions of marketing. Business, and specifically marketing, includes many social institutions which are important influences on the value of society. Because marketing is so significant to society, the question of social goals and social responsibility inevitably must be faced. It business does not establish its own social goals and design programmes to achieve those social goals, it is certainty that society will fill the void. There inevitably are social functions of business in contemporary society. Eells and Walton have suggested four social functions.[9] these are functions which concern marketing management and which should be considered by marketing scientists. Each function has marketing overtones; the functions can be perceived as the social functions of marketing.

Survival

This may be the basic and the ultimate goal of a business and the prime measure of marketing activity. Profits are both a prerequisite for survival and a test of survivability; service is the road to customer satisfactions and, therefore, to survival in a competitive economic climate. Social responsibility is probably a necessary condition of survival over the long run. Many marketing strategies can be designed to achieve the survival goal. Questions about the strategies of growth, institutional survival, subsidies, and institutional and enterprise abandonment, are in part ethical questions.

Profit Making

A business is the only human organisation whose existence depends on profit. As Eells and Walton point out, governments, can tax, churches can call on members for support, and the family can survive without profits. But a business requires profits to justify its existence. Profit making is a basic goal of business and the profit concept underlies marketing. Profit goals are achieved in the marketplace, and the basic task of the marketing manager is to serve consumer needs profitably in a way which will be consistent with long-range survival goals.

The are many ethical aspects to questions about business goals, such as the following:

Growth of the firm of a division a product lien or a product.

Short-term profit maximization.

Profit maximization over the long run.

Service to the country, society, and the common good.

Service to customers.

Enlargement of size of market.

Maintenance or increase in share of market.

Establishment of an image for the firm, division or product.

Diversification of corporate activity.

Achievement of industry leadership.

Development of reputation and stature of management.

Employee welfare and satisfactions.

Securing a balance between government and domestic business.

Securing a balance between domestic and foreign business.

Making the firm a satisfying one for employees and managers.

Maintaining employment at certain levels in particular plants.

Minimizing risk of government antitrust enforcement activities.

The length of the list may suggest that goal setting is not a simple matter or that it can be undertaken on purely factual terms.

Service

Business has service functions to perform in addition to profit making. Timothy E. Shea, vie President in charge of Engineering of Western Electric Company, has said, "Business is a vehicle through which man serves society." Such a view of service and profits requires a balancing of functions by managers. Customer service is one of the keys to survival and profit. The serving of customer needs profitably is the basis concern of marketing executives. Service to customers and to society concepts rests on an ethical view of business practice.

Social Responsibility

Another social function of business is the obligation of a firm to meet its social responsibilities to its employees, the community, and the public, as well as to its owners and customers.

Social responsibilities are those of corporate good citizenship in a society. Sometimes social and economic goals and the functions required to perform them may being conflict. More often, in the long run, enlightened self-interest and the corporate sense of social responsibility coincide. When they do not, managers acting as both businessmen and citizens attempt to reconcile conflicts knowing that failure to do so may mean additional government regulation.

Business itself is a social instrumentality of society designed to facilitate the achievement of given ends. Marketing, or any business function, is a corporate activity designed to achieve given objectives. The genius of American business is that through the marketing system consumers are offered an infinite variety of goods and services from which they can choose those which will best enable free individuals to approach fulfilling their own view of the good life. Critics of marketing frequently neglect the point that the pursuit of the good life may be largely an individual matter and that restrictions on selling effort almost always result in restrictions on the buyers' freedom to choose and act.

A business manager is, of course, concerned with the social view of business problems just as he is concerned with the economic environment in which the firm operates. But the operating manager is primarily concerned with other problems, such as managing marketing activity in order to achieve particular corporate goals in a market society. As such, he tends to see social and economic areas not as ends in themselves but as environmental restraints on corporate activity or as areas of marketing opportunity. However, top management does have as one of its major challenges the job of answering the question whether a free market economy can provide social welfare with individual freedom as it meets the material needs of free consumers. This is a difficult and complex question; the Degree of success of business executives in answering it will, to a large extent, determine the future of the free enterprise system.

Business executives are aware that strategies to fulfill these social functions have varying levels of ethical acceptability. It is interesting to consider the relationship between the acceptability level and profit returns. Simon has suggested that ethical considerations can be introduced into computer programmed business games and that the higher the acceptability level, the less the profit return to the alernative.[10] There does not seem to be any computer business game which at present has built into it a set of strategies, opportunities, and tactics that would have varying degrees of moral acceptability as judged by our business society. It is possible to build into a game strategies or varying degrees of moral acceptability which would have payoffs attached corresponding to the payoffs they might produce in the real world. Simon suggests such acts ad "gouging customers in an emergency, moving out of a small town precipitately cutting off established dealers, and using unfair sources of information." Players in such a game could be told that they would be judged as both profit makers and as ethical businessmen. As Simon put it, they would not be necessarily be told what calculus, if any, is used to make ethics and profits commensurable. The real world does not offer any such calculus as an accurate guide to ethical costs. Possibly players will be told that not only their scores but their particular ethical acts would be publicized to the other players in the game. An interesting line of experimentation is opened up by such suggestions.

On a pragmatic basis it is possible to relate the level of ethical expectations of a society to the negative control of government regulation of business. In a complex industrial society it is government which sets the legal boundaries and enforces the rules of business conduct. Their rules do much to mold the environment of business and the climate in which marketing decisions are made. In marketing terms it can be said that the consumer is the controller of a firm's destiny. But on a broader scale, it is the government, representing public consensus, which exercises the ultimate control over business. In some societies the government is more important than the market as the dominating mechanism of society a prime function of decision makers then becomes the management of policies and conditions which will minimize public demands for regulation of business. But the ultimate case for ethical behaviour does not rest on these grounds, although such might be an acceptable form of corporate rationalization of efforts better ethical levels. Efforts to still or neutralize the voices of protest are not the reasons. Perhaps it is than the business of business is to service society – and that this is difficult, if not impossible, unless the ethical norms of society are understood and fulfilled, and over the long run, perhaps exceeded.

Integrating Ethics and Science in Marketing

The anticipation of tomorrow is one of the major concern of managers, and a function of marketing scientists is to help marketing managers anticipate the future. Thus marketing scientists are concerned with the subject of changing moral values of society. All concerned with advancing science in marketing must understand the nature of the rising standards of ethical expectations of business on the part of the pubic. To ignore these would be as unwise as to ignore changing educational, income or other levels of consumer expectations or behaviour. The integration science and ethics can today be questioned on the grounds that it means mix of rational scientific information (facts) with moral judgments. However, the trends of history seem to indicate the promise of a greater degree of integration between these two cultural approaches to the problems of meeting man's material needs. The hope is not inconsistent with scientific method.

One step toward science-ethics-management integration is to be aware of the problem of relating moral and ethical considerations to marketing practice. Another step is to ponder, study, and research the area of ethical and marketing science relationships. Perhaps what is called for is experimentation with new approaches which will enable us to overcome existing barriers to communication and understanding between cultural representatives. This is a hoped-for outcome of the meta-marketing approach as it might fuse marketing science and theory, management policy, and social philosophy to meet the challenges of the scientific revolution.

-- *Eugene J. Kelley*

REFERENCES

1. James W. Culliton, "The Problem of Ethics in Business," in Ethics in Business, Robert Bartels (ed.), Bureau of Business Research, Columbus, Ohio, 1963, p. 9.! Comprehensive forty-three page annotated bibliography on the general subject of ethics in business is included in this book.

2. *New York Times* (February 16, 1964.).

3. Robert Ferber, Donald F. Blankertz, and Sidney Hollander, Jr., *Marketing Research*, Ronald Press, New York, 1964, p. 602.

4. Theodore Levitt, "Dangers of Social Responsibility," *Harvard Business Review*, Vol. XXXVI (September 1958), pp. 41-60).

5. Morton White, The Age of Analysis, *The New American Library*, New York, 65, p. 217.

6. Francis X. Kane, "Security Is too Important to be Left to Computers," Fortunt, Vol. LXIX, No 4, (April 1964), p. 147.

7. Robert Bartels, "A Methodological Framework for Comparative Marketing Study," In *Toward Scientific Marketing*, Stephen A. Greyset (ed.), Proceedings of the 1963 Winter Conference of the American Marketing Association, Chicago, 1964, p. 383.

8. Kenneth E. Boulding, "General Systems Theory – The Skeleton of Science," Management Science (April 1956). See also the discussion in William Laser and Engene J. Kelley, *Interdisciplinary contributions to Marketing Management*, Bureau of Business Research, E. Lansing, Michigan, 1959, pp. 1-31.

9. Richard Eells and Clarence Walton, *Conceptual Foundations of Business*, Richard D. Irwin, Inc., Homewood, III, 1961, pp. 432-33.

10. J.L. Simon, "How Do Beliefs Affect Business Performance?" (Unpublished manuscript, Urbana, Illinois, 1963, p. 36). For a report on an empirical study of business ethics see Raymond C. Baumhart, "How Ethical Are Businessmen?" *Harvard Business Review*, Vol. XXXIX (July-August 1961), p. 6.

9

MANAGING MARKETING EFFORT

Competitive pressure compel a firm to become a market-oriented mechanism. Three fundamental concepts are offered as a foundation for a marketing viewpoint. First, all thinking about the firm should being with the market–actual and potential. Second, the future of a firm is more important than the present, for it is the future that presents the opportunity for innovation. Third, commitment to adaptive change is the key to profit optimization. A comparison of marketing and production viewpoints is presented.

Hear the Message of the Market Place

For the past several years, the "marketing point of view" has probably been the most popular recurring topic at professional, trade association and company meetings. As a result, many companies and their managers have accepted a superficial commitment to market-mined thinking. They often lack, however, a clear understanding of what is involved for their organisations. In time, they are likely to become discouraged with results, and they may even abandon what could be the most profitable administrative change their firms could introduce.

It is important, therefore, to ask what is meant by the term "marketing viewpoint. What is its proper role in management planning and action? How can it be introduced and put to work effectively? What benefits should be anticipated?

The place to start answering these questions is not the office of the marketing vice president. Rather, it is the office of the president, the man responsible for formulating and executing a the general management function in his business.

The general management function is the brain of a business—the guiding control. It determines principal goals and organizes there sources to achieve them. It designs the policies that define a firm's character and the strategies and tactics that follow. Inevitably, therefore, the way a general manager view his business must have a strong influence on how that business is run and how it performs.

The significance of this point has not been clearly grasped in many proposals to give the marketing function greater attention. To say that marketing needs more emphasis is superficial. What managers really need is a new way of looking at their organisation, an ability to see in the familiar business a wholly different character than they formerly observed and perhaps took for granted.

This is the kind of fresh viewpoint that in the 1920's saw the opportunity to launch the Sears, Roebuck and the Montgomery ward mail-order firms into general merchandise retailing on a national scale. It is the viewpoint that in the 1930's grasped the potential of self-service grocery stores and proceeded to revolutionize the retailing of food. Te same innovative outlook is now beginning to use the grocery supermarket for distributing a variety of non-food items. Another example is offered by the successful attack of the discount house in the 1950's on the traditional high markup, full-service retailing of household appliances.

This is the kind of management imagination that sees in the computer not simply a high-powered clerical machine but an information processing tool that can change techniques of decision-making and help to displace management art and hunch with a rational, quantitative approach to the solution of comp[illegible] problems.

We can best see the significance of this revolution in management thinking if we contrast two basic ways of looking at a business.

The first—which dominated management thinking through the initial phase of the industrial revolution—sees the firm primarily as a producing organism.

Management attention is focused on engineering and manufacturing problems. The drive for efficiency identifies production as the place to reduce costs. It presses to simplify product design, substitute cheaper materials, mechanize work operations, replace batch with continuous-flow processes. Most recently, the thrust is to automate manufacturing activities. In this setting, efforts to innovate are directed principally toward improving existing products and processes. In short, management sees direct relation between cost cutting and profits, and acts accordingly. Marketing is not, of course, ignored in this management view. But the sales function is treated largely as an effort to find customers for the output of the plant. Marketing costs are regarded as a necessary evil—as expenses rather than investment. The are dealt with as if they were passive influences in the total array of business activities. One common result of this attitudes is that marketing budgets tend to be established in relation to revenue, usually as a predetermined percentage of present or forecast sales.

A contrasting way of looking at a business sees the firm primarily as a marketing organism.

Question to Answer

Here, management's view looks outward toward the customer. The important questions to be answered before making policy or investment decisions are: who are the present and potential customers? Where do they live and buy? What are their purchase habits and preferences, and why? What needs are served by the company's products and services? What important needs are not adequately served? What is the state of competition? The market share? The trends? The prospects? What sales potentials are suggested by evolving economic and social developments? Out of the answers to these questions come the data for investment, research, engineering and production decisions, as well as the design of marketing programmes.

Production and engineering are not ignored in this management view. But it treats the manufacturing function and everything related to it as resources to be used in designing and delivering the most profitable responses to the challenges and opportunities of the market. Expenditures for marketing activities are seen as investments. They are determined flexibly in relation to profit potentials, rather than rigidly as ratios of costs to sales.

The history of the introduction of scientific management techniques clearly reveals the dominance of the production-centered view in management thinking throughout the first half of this century. What we call scientific management was designed for the control of manufacturing. Time and motion study, cost analysis, budgeting, mathematical rules for decision-making, in fact every advance from art to science in administration occurred initially in production. Scientific management in marketing has lagged by at least one generation. It is only since about 1950 that any lively interest has appeared in applying the new management techniques to marketing.

A Pervasive influence

The Marketimg-centered view of a businessinfluences every aspect of management.

Consider, for example, the policies that govern decisions about variety in a product line. In contrast to the simplicity urged by the production view, the marketing view recommends diversity to meet the full range of customers' wants and needs. The production manager's concept of an ideal world is one in which a single product--one design, one size, one colour--moves uninterruptedly down the manufacturing line. This minimize all product costs; tooling, setup, instruction and supervision of workers, scheduling of work flow, ordering of raw materials, investment in inventories. The marketing manager's contrasting concept is one in which no customer ever has to be told he cannot have what he wants.

The historical dominance of the production view has been assisted by solid evidence (in accounting records) of costs attributable to product variety. Marketing HAS BEEN Weakened by the inability to trace an identifiable cost to an order unfilled shipment delayed because of a narrow product line or a thin inventory.

The production view presses for retaining old products for which tooling, materials and knowledge are established. The marketing view presses for discarding old products in favour of improved models, or designing new products to serve customers' needs more precisely, or gaining an advance on competitors.

The production view, in short, is cost-oriented. The marketing view is revenue-oriented.

The production view cherishes stability. The marketing view welcomes and encourages change and innovation.

The production view approaches pricing decisions from the expense side. The marketing view approaches them from the revenue side. The production view asks: "

How much will it cost to make this?" The marketing view asks: "How much will we make if we sell this?"

The marketing view sees the present through the eyes of the future.

At the general management level the two views must, of course, be brought into balance and tested against the profit criterion. A total surrender to the marketing view could lead to a galloping case of policies growth. Nevertheless, the dynamic competitive pressures of our economy increasingly complain approach to the profit balance by way of the marketing viewpoint. This amounts to a prescription to look at a business first as a market-oriented mechanism. Production considerations can be surveyed later on the way to a summary assessment of investment, cost, risk and profit.

This changed viewpoint can be brought about even in along

established industry, like railroading. The Southern Pacific, for example, has long been acclaimed for defining its business mission as the provision of transportation, not only railroad services. Another road, the Southern, has recently been applauded by observers for its creative, revenue-and-profit-conscious attack on the complex proems of fright rates.

A comparable change is being accomplished in some equipment manufacturing companies that have broadened their operations from selling individual machines to designing and marketing integrated materials handling and processing systems, under automated control.

When the marketing view takes precedence in top management thinking, the business is often seen in a new way. One of the most dramatic examples of this fresh view is the recognition that research and development can be applied in marketing as usefully and as profitably as in production. A retail chain may use one unit as an experimental laboratory for studying lay out, traffic flow, merchandise display or prices. A manufacturing company with national distribution may use one territory as a research area in which experiments are conducted on marketing methods, sales promotion techniques or customer services. New types of advertising, new copy slants or a new package are tested "guinea pig" audiences before major investment commitments are made.

In this way, the information required for a profitable approach to servicing dynamic consumer demand can become the first input to management thinking about every aspect of the business. Out of such studies come guidelines for engineering and product research. Out of these studies, too, come ideas for innovation in distribution techniques. Products maybe profitably sold in retail stores or through industrial middlemen previously not in the marketing stream. Novel packaging ideas, such as containers with secondary household uses, may be evolved. Now services or financing arrangements may be developed. Research on competitive practices and consumer demand may throw light on pricing decisions and encourage managers to break the shackles of cost-plus pricing.

More Innovation

The primacy of a marketing viewpoint is likely to be left in other areas, as well. It encourages planning and location inventories to meet customer requirements rather than production convenience. If favours scheduling a profit rather than a cost criterion.

Above all, leadership from the marketing viewpoint sees the future as a source of profitable opportunities ready for exploitation by imaginative management. It fears the changing circumstances that threaten investment in manufacturing facilities which may be obsolete before their useful life has been exhausted.

How can the marketing viewpoint be brought into a position of dominance in general management thinking?

There is no single, simple answer to this question. Installing an experienced marketing manager as chief executive officer will not be effective if his principal associates in research, production and finance do not change the way they look at the business. Redesigning the organisation chart to bring more marketing managers into the policy-making arena may encourage divisive factionalism and delay in planning and executing programmes.

What is required is no less than a comprehensive turn-around of the thinking, of the total mental set of all top-level managers. Such a transformation will do more than affect the shaping of policy at the organization's peak. It will also help to thrust the new ideas down through the layers of the line organization.

The head of one large corporation attacked the problem by hiring an our side consultant to study the company's weak market position in one part of its diversified product line and recommend a new approach He then used the consultant's radical marketing proposals as a target for interdepartmental study by working groups at several levels. From vice presidents down to middle managers in the line organization, with an assignment to examine every implication of the recommended programme for engineered, production and finance. The outcome was an amended programme to which all functions were committed. The new marketing approach was then put into operation. Its successful performance in revenues, profits and strengthened competitive position led to queries about the possibility of study other parts of the product line in the same way. In the president's view, the evolving experience, building step by step, is demonstrably encouraging an active interest in marketing potential and requirements throughout his management group.

Another company is trying a different roue toward the same objective. Outstanding divisional managers in every part of the business are begin assigned planned tours of duty in the marketing department. Here they work not as observers but as responsible line executive. Early results make the president confident that the value of a marketing viewpoint is being properly appreciated in all pars of the management team.

Whatever the approach, the job must be viewed as a comprehensive educational effort. What we know about the educational process tells to that it is slow, that it builds strength through reinforcement of theory in practice, that it needs both precept and example. No simple policy pronouncement of the "we have entered new era' variety can do more than delude the gullible and inflame the naive within a management group.

10

THE FORMULATION OF A MARKET STRATEGY

If business management is to become more scientific, the firm's objectives must first be clearly stated. This is essential, since formulating marketing strategy involves the definition of the firm's broad objectives and the translation of these into marketing objectives. After this has been done, marketing targets must be set, and the appropriate marketing mix to achieve these targets must be selected.

Business management has been called many things: it commonly is described as an art; some describe it as a guessing game. Perhaps the height of wisdom on his subject is contained in the phrase, "business is business," for business is not like anything else. Clearly, success as a business executive requires what some people describe as "artistry" and intuition – though these probably are far less vital than just plain luck. In addition, in this paper endeavours to prove, successful business management demands careful and maximum application of the scientific method.

The scientific method obviously needs no defense; only an eccentric will maintain that guesses are more valid bases for decision than careful observation and experimentation. However, the phases of business management that are amenable to scientific methods are far from obvious.

Is There a Science of Business Management?

Little is to be gained by pointing a finger at businessmen for having managerial decision-making in a relatively primitive state until recently while production men applied the fruits of science to achieve miracles in the factory. The very large number of business failures and high turnover among business executives have been punishment enough. However, the contrast between the methods by which managerial and production decisions are made deserves emphasis, for there exists an influential body of executives—and some academicians—who find the main ingredient of business success to be "good judgement and practice of the managerial art." These phrases are question begging unless one is able to define what is meant by good judgment and the managerial art. Moreover, such as view deprecates the importance of fact-gathering, rigorous reasoning, hypothesis-testing—and all elements of the scientific method that can be applied to many of the problems faced by businessmen.

It may appear pretentious to link business management with the scientific method. When one speaks of "scientific management" or "scientific marketing" he simply means that business decisions should have the maximum benefit of factual support, close rigorous reasoning, and empirical test; also, that every conclusion reached should be open to challenge and be capable of rational defense. There is no room in this concept for bowing to authority, deference to the intuitions or experience" of older men or persons associated with the business for a longer time; it requires that decisions be made on the basis of facts and logical argument rather than by appeal to authority.

No one familiar with business dreams that it will become an "exact science" which rest upon a body of proved principles analogous to what has been produced by the chemist and physicist. Everyone knows that duplicable experiments cannot be the main technique employed for arriving at generalizations applicable to business. The methods available to business executives for solving concrete problems are, at bet, relatively crude, unreliable and unproved by the standards of most physical sciences. However, the year vastly more reliable than reliance on hunch, intuitions, feel and guesses, or appeal to authority.

The scientific method, or the most scientific techniques applicable to business—however one prefers to express it—is not to be confused with the use of the conference or committee method of decision-making. All too often, these methods are applied in a manner that brings several uninformed people together to pool their thoughts and hammer out a common agreement. A "bull session," no matte by what elegant title it may be dignified, will not produce valuable results unless at least some participant are very well informed. Once maximum use is made of observation and experimentation, discussion will generally prove very valuable; however, it certainly cannot substitute for the collection and analysis of facts.

Practitioners in most fields—especially those who practice for a fee—understandably are anxious to persuade others that their fields of specialization are sciences. Only recently, however, have some person specializing are sciences. Only recently, however, have some persons specializing in business fields claimed to be "applied" scientists. To understand that they claim, one must also know what they disavow. Almost all admit their inability to remotely approach the accuracy, predictability and even objectivity of most physical sciences. But they maintain that there do exist data, methods of data collection, experimental and testing procedures, and methods of analyzing and testing findings whose application to business would greatly increase the proportion of correct managerial decisions. Rather than great accuracy in absolute terms, these people claim to be relatively accurate in a field where attempts at systematic and rigorous answers to problems remain exceptional.

How can Business Management be made more Scientific?

To make business management into an applied science, executives, must first clarify their firm's objectives. Although the selection of ultimate business objectives is necessarily unscientific, for they express the fundamental values f individuals who establish broad policy, operating objectives stated fully, clearly, and concretely are indispensable if one is to make managerial decision-making amenable to the scientific method. Once objectives are known, the selection of means becomes the task of appraising, by the best means available, the relative effectiveness of alternatives.

A Statement of a Firm's Broad Objectives. Business objectives can be stated on a variety of levels; one must begin with the ultimate—the broadest and most general—and work back to the more narrow and specific ends that they imply. The two most widely expressed ultimate objectives of corporate management these days are: first, to make maximum profits for the firm over the life of the enterprise and strictly within the limits of the law; and, second, to conduct operations in a manner that gives equal weight to the claims of; stockholders, labour, consumers and government. Both of these broad objectives must be translated into more specific market goals if they are to be very helpful to executives responsible for making concrete business decisions.

Statement of Market Objectives. In pursuit of maximum profits, for example, management might set its operating objectives at: a maximum of dollar or unit sales; a maximum share of total or of particular geographic markets; maximum profit figured as a percentage of net worth or of sales; it might set itself the objective of a steadily increasing return on sales or profits; or the goal of an increasing market share. Bt even if narrowed this far, the objectives are not as helpful as they can be made. It is possible to state market objectives in a form that facilitates an application of the scientific method.

Market objectives are best expressed as customer types—narrowly defined—whose patronage the business will try especially to win. (Of course, it will not turn away others desiring to buy.) Once objectives have been refined to this on, management is in a position to formulate more specific problems in a manner that makes it readily amenable to solution by the scientific method:

A determination of the types of customers the firm should try to service in particular does not flow simply and logically.

from a firm's ultimate objectives. A careful consideration of alternative markets must underline the selection of those markets to be cultivated intensively.

Concept of a "Market Strategy"

Put differently, use of "scientific" methods for making marketing decisions calls for what is here termed a "market strategy," The main purpose of this paper is to explain what a market strategy consists of and how it can serve as a potent organizing tool for the decisions of business executives. It may well assist students of marketing by giving a central structure to various facets of the study of business.

A market strategy consists of two parts: (1) the definition of market targets—selecting the types of customers whose patronage will be sought; and (2) the "composition of a marketing mix"—picking a combination of sales promotion devices that will be employed. Market targets represent the operating objectives (which are subject to change of curse) of top management; the marketing mix represents a combination of instruments by which these objectives are pursued.

The scientific method finds its greatest potential application to marketing by calling for a rigorous appraisal of the relative effectiveness of alternative means of winning the patronage of particular types of potential customers. The scientific marketer must assemble the best evidence available, determine what additional evidence should be gathered, subject all information collected to rigorous analysis, formulate and test hypotheses regarding the effect on unit sales of such things as: price changes, changes in the quality of the product, advertising outlays, number of salesmen, margins offered retailers, number of retail outlets, etc.

It will be acknowledged at the outset that no generalizations about these matters can be applied to all or even to many products. Answers to specific marketing problems probably differ for each individual business—and will not even be stable for it over long periods of time. Thus, top management must reconcile itself to an unending study of the relative effectiveness of sales promotion devices. An agreement's success in achieving the market a targets it sets itself will, it is maintained here, depend upon the scientific rigor with which it conducts this endless study—rather than upon the artistry and intuition of its top executives.

The steps involved in the formulation of a market strategy will be discussed in broad general terms in this paper. First, the determination of market targets will be taken up; thereupon, the composition of a marketing mix will be discussed.

Definition of Market Targets. No one can hope to please everybody! Person who attempt to win the friendship of everyone are likely to have few friends, for they will lack individuality and basic personality.

Many will doubt their sincerity and almost everyone will get an uneasy feeling in their presence and think that there is something "fishy" about them. Businesses who try to sell to everybody risk a similar fate. If they attempt to convince their prestige conscious customers that their product represents the highest possible quality and the brand that customers buy if they do not have to worry about cost, they may repel potential customers who are extremely concerned about economy But, if they claim that the product represents both the highest possible quality and the lower price, they will be believed by almost no one.

No business needs to sell to all potential customers. A fraction of the total market is all any firm need hope for—and the Department of Justice frowns on those wit more ambitious hopes. IT IS Almost always wise for a management to select consciously the types of customers it will try to win as their firm's main patrons; in so doing, management can mobilize the full resources of the firm to a clearly defined task. To make such a selection, management should first divide the total potential market into its "significant segments.

Potential customers must be divided into groups that have some significance from the standpoint of what management can and should do about them. The most important criteria for segmenting the market for any product are: (1) strength of their need or desire for the product: (2) channels (media, distribution outlet, etc.) through which they can be reached; (3) "appeals" (lines of argûment) to which they are responsive; (4) degrees of responsiveness to particular types of sales appear (that is, their ability to be influenced by price considerations, availability of credit, sales talk of salesmen, etc.); and (5) physical location.

The most significant market segments vary widely from product to product. Customers must be classified according to the many special features of the product in question and of the circumstances under which it is sold. In almost every case, however, there are two types of criteria that should be employed: the first are the features traditionally used by market analysts. These generally can be measured and include such things as: incomes, marital status, size of family, religion age, size of community, whether or not the product is already owned, the age and condition of the product owned, etc. The second are social and psychological characteristics that almost always are unmeasurable and apply particularly to the product in question. For example, one might divide potential customers of most products into: the self-confident and those who are unsure of themselves; the adventurous and those craving the familiar; the ostentatious and the modest, etc. In addition, particular attitudes are confronted in the marketing of some products but have no being upon others. For example, it seems to have been established that the use of instant coffee is associated in the minds of many housewives with neglect of a wife's proper duties. This attitude is not likely to have any bearing upon the sale of women's hats, however.

As already indicated, the criteria by which potential customers are divided should meet two tests; (1) they should reflect differences which indicate or affect the actions that businessmen should take in trying to win their patronage; and (2) they should apply to the particular product in the specific markets in which they are being sold. In classifying potential customers, one should err, if at all, in the direction of dividing them into too many rather than too few groups. Both measurable and unmeasurable characteristics should be combined into one scheme of classification. It is likely that one will end up with many scores of market segments; as stated the more the better.

Those segments should then be scrutinized carefully to determine; (1) which ones are least adequately served at present: (2) those which the particular firm is best qualified to attract—because of its product, personnel, tradition, reputation, standing in the customer's mind, etc.; and (3) those that management would like to make the core of the business over the future, simply on grounds of personal taste.

By scrutinizing the total potential market broken down into segments possessing significance for action, a management may well find that several parts of the market had gone relatively uncovered. It so, it may profit by cultivating those particular markets, using measures especially effective in winning their patronage.

Management should also select the market segments to cultivate intensively by matching its own resources against what is needed to "sell" particular types of prospective customers. Special qualities about a firm's management, location, past performance, design of product. Company tradition, etc. may make it particularly effective in serving certain market segments. To match the firm against market segments involves a realistic appraisal of the firm's strengths and weakness and of the factors that influence the purchase of each potential customer group. Often a firm will find itself especially suited to win patronage from particular types of customers—which may also be actively cultivated by some of its competitors. Not infrequently, there is a conflict between market targets that are an covered and those for which the firm has special talent. A choice must be made, and often it will not be an easy one.

Businessmen are people! They have likes and dislikes that do and should influence their decisions. The most profitable markets may be found in regions which require location in uncomfortable climates or uncongenial social environments. In part, a selection of market segments for intensive cultivation must be influenced by such considerations. However, management cannot long follow its inclinations if they would result in persistent losses.

To summarize what has been said upto this point, a scientific market strategy first requires that a business formulate general and broad objectives. These must then be translated into operating objectives, by specifying the particular market segments the firm will cultivate most intensively.

To make such a decision, which is among he most crucial that management must make, requires an exhaustive division of all potential customers into segments which possess marketing significance—that is, they are best cultivated in different ways. The selection of the particular segments that the firm should cultivate intensively should be made on grounds of the extent to which they are being neglected at present, the special qualifications that the firm possesses to serve them and the taste of the business owners.

Composition of the Marketing Mix. Once the firm's market targets have been specified, management faces the task of selecting measures most likely to achieve them. In modern marketing parlance, we must discuss the "marketing mix."

The "marketing mix" is composed of large battery of devices which might be employed to induce customers to buy a particular product. The same devises are involved whether one is of thinking of inducing altogether new buyers to purchase the product or of shifting customers from rival bands to one's own. These devices are here termed" sales promotion devices "and include a wide variety of instruments. It is wise to list separately those which are at the disposal of manufactures and those which may be employed by distributors and dealers.

Sales promotion devices that might be used by manufactures to induce customers to buy their products include such things as: quality of product, special product features, amount of advertising outlays, lines of advertising outlays, lines of advertising appeals employed, types of advertising media used, number of personal salesmen employed, quality f salesmen, distributive channels employed, quality of distributors used, number of distributions, location of sales effort (geographically), product guarantees, servicing arrangements, credit and accommodations supplied.

Distributors and dealers might use the following instruments to induce customers to patronize them; price inducements, advertising, number and quality of salesmen, location, air conditioning, location of merchandise departments in the store, breadth of selection offered customers, width of aisles, hours of operation, return privileges, credit accommodation, delivery service, etc.

Even though the foregoing lists of sales promotion devices are far from complete, they are long. And, what is especially significant, management must make decisions regarding almost every one of them. Either consciously or by default, a management decides whether or not to employ each device and in what form and to what degree.

Although a firm may concentrate on one particular sales promotion device, it almost invariably employs many of them to some degree. Even firms which rely primarily upon the appeal of low price must d some advertising; if they were not to do so, their low price offerings might not be noticed by many customers. Moreover, they are generally compelled to give some assurance of acceptable quality (by guarantees or return privileges). The point urged here is that each firm must employ a combination of sales promotion devices, rather than only one, and that the overriding task of marketing management consists in selecting the optimum combination. The formulation of a combination of sales promotion devices is sometimes described as the "Composition of a marketing mix" for an actual firm.

1. The selection of a marketing mix must be made very explicitly in terms of the particular market segments whose patronage is to be sought most intensively.
2. To a considerable degree, the individual sales promotion devices are substitutes for one another. One could spend more on advertising or to hire personal salesmen of higher

quality, or to build more quality into the product, etc.

3. Almost every one of the possible sales promotion devices must be employed in some form ad to some degree. No single line of appeal for patronage will suffice.
4. In deciding how much to rely upon each sales promotion device, the following general rules should be applied:
   (a) Never expend sums for sales promotion unless you anticipate that they will produce enough additional revenue to cover all of the costs incurred to obtain that revenue—including the sales promotion outlay. (One must take account of the effect of a sales promotion outlay on future sales as well as their immediate impact.)
   (b) Compare alternative sales promotion devices that might be employed to obtain any specified increase in sales volume and employ that one which involves least cost.

Connection Between "Scientific Marketing" and Market Strategy

Executives with responsibility in the marketing area will find maximum opportunity to apply the scientific method if they consciously endeavour to formulate a concrete market strategy. Preferably, this formulation will take a written form, and be quite explicit and detailed. A market strategy combines explicit ends and the means selected to achieve them; the scientific method can be employed to a considerable degree to assess the effectiveness of alternative measures for attaining any given objective.

Specifically, top marketing executives will be entitled to regard themselves as 'scientific' if they carry out the following steps:

1. Formulate each problem clearly and sharply, and in a form that lends itself to maximum verification by the use of evidence.
2. Gather available evidence bearing on the problem.

3. Arrange for the collection of additional information that would contribute to a solution to the problem—within the financial means of the firm.
4. Organize and analyze the information gathered in a manner that will shed maximum light on the solution to the original problem.
5. Formulate conclusions suggested by the evidence into hypotheses, such of which implies a potential solution to the original problem.
6. Test the hypotheses to the fullest extent possible.
7. Make a list of alternative solutions to the problem that has been discarded in favour of the one selected.

Historical Antecedents of the Marketing Strategy Concept

When a new concept stands by itself, its meaning and significance often are unclear. It contrasted with other views and seen as part of a general progression of ideas, it generally can be understood and appraised rather easily. Accordingly, the notions which preceded the marketing strategy concept will be described very briefly. Historians recording the process of intellectual discovery invariably conclude that thought develops in an orderly, step-by-step method. Whether this view is valid or is the creation of the historian themselves sometimes is unclear. Consequently, the following sketch of the marketing strategy concept's development may not describe how individuals came by their idea; it does, however describe the state of thinking at successive points in time.

The marketing strategy concept attempts to organize the factors that determine the sales of individual products. We must therefore seek its antecedents among the writings of men who were interested in explaining or actually influencing the volume of sales. The earliest probably would be the merchants of ancient times and the early Green philosophers who occasionally wrote about commercial affairs. Given the modest purposes at hand, this review will pass over the early writings and will start with the "Classical" economists.

Although they doubtless knew that they were oversimplifying the matter, classical economists based their explanations of sales solely on the effect of price. (All other possible influences were held constant and left unexplored.) They offered a simple and monolithic view of the determination of sales that was later incorporated into the demand schedule. In their view, sales varied inversely with price—at any given time and with all other things remaining equal; later economists summarized the relationship between sales and price in the "law of Demand."

The second stage in the attempts of professional economists to explain the determinants of sales might be dated from the publication of Edward Chamberlin's "theory of Monopolistic Competition."[1] It was during this stage that academic economists first took explicit account of non price influences n sales. Professor Chamberlin explored the effects of advertising on sales and explained this factor in the traditional manner common to formal economics. Despite the fact that the "Theory of Monopolistic Competition" was written over a quarter of a century ago, many academic discussions of sales still proceed as if price were the overwhelmingly important determinant of sales. Little attention is devoted even now to non price influences on sales by economists, although several books have been written by academic economists on the subject of individual nonprice influences on sales.

At this stage, the development of concepts to explain product sales reached a fork in the road. One prong continued the application of traditional techniques to take account of a larger number of influences on sales. An important step in this direction was taken in 1941 when Professor Kenneth Boulding2 treated sales efforts and costs in the same way that theorists had handled production costs; this theoretical framework contained the implicit analogy between the to marketing executive and the engineer. Economists have not built on this major breakthrough, however. An article by P.J. Verdoorn in 19563 represents perhaps the high point of this line of development, which is characterized by the use of geometric tools of analysis.

Further developments along this traditional route are in the hands of persons with a mathematical orientation. The field of operations research known as "programming" handles many sales promotion activities without serious difficulty, because mathematics is vastly more powerful than geometry. Programming of sales activity is not being explored by formal economics but represents the contribution of marketing specialists in the main.

The second fork in the road reached after the writing of the "Theory of Monopolistic Competition" might be termed the checklist approach to the sales problem. It was along this road that the term "marketing mix" was introduced for the first time by Professor Neil Borden in approximately 1953.[4] Writers who have followed this route were concerned with two major factors: First, they sought to itemize the large number of influences upon sales that marketing executives must take into account; second, they were interested in facilitating practical application of the concept to concrete operating problems. Foremost among the writers who adopted this approach were Professors Neil Bordenand Albert Frey,[5] The latter attempted to relate the marketing mix concept directly to the development of marketing programmes in his publication, which carries the subtitle, "Programming for Optimum Results."

With the development of the checklist approach, the enormity of the problem confronting the top marketing executive became apparent. The task of balancing a very large umber of variables (even if one ignores their interdependence) clearly is huge. Paucity of evidence about the productivity of individual sales promotion devices, and the difference between present and future markets inevitably makes the task of the chief marketing executive overwhelming, if not impossible. The inability to see down a workable method of composing a marketing mix is not a failing of the concept itself; the concept does describe what the top marketing executive should attempt to do. It certainly represents a substantial improvement over earlier views that took explicit account of only a few factors influencing sales. The complexity of the sale function is real and not a figment of the imagination of the concept builders.

Doctrine discussing determinants of sales had reached this state when the concept of marketing strategy was first set down in 1957. This concept differs form earlier thought on the subject by relating customer targets directly to the marketing mix. (It may be regarded as another step done with road from the checklist approach to the sales problem). It emphasizes that an effective marketing mix requires top management to be explicit about the kinds of customers to whom the business is trying to sell because specific sales promotion devices that appeal to some customer will bore others and even repel some.

The addition of customer targets to the concept of the marketing mix partly overcomes the difficulties in implementing the concept caused by a lack of information. When a marketing specialist is explicit. About his target customers and informs himself thoroughly about their needs, desires, perceptions, habits, attitudes, assumptions, economic situation, etc. He can guess more confidently about the productivity of different sales promotion devices than if he thinks in terms of so unrealistic and abstraction as "the average customer."

The marketing strategy concept also directed attention to a major omission in the thinking of many business executives. When the marketing strategy concept was reduced to writing, even as today, the greatest marketing errors resulted from the failure of sellers to be explicit and selective about customer targets.

The concept of marketing strategy certainly does not represent the pinnacle of thought about the determinants of sales. It is intended primarily for businessmen who must make operating decisions—rather than is mathematicians or econometricians. Superior methods of formulating the sales problem are certain to be developed. Nevertheless, this view of sales determination may explain the sales and marketing function more clear and suggest how to deal with it more effectively than did earlier views.

REFERENCES

1. Harvard University Press, Cambridge, Massachusetts, 1933.

2. See his *Economic Analysis*, Harpers, 1941

3. See his "Marketing form the Producer's Point of View," *Journal of Marketing*, January 1956.

4. Professor Borden first introduced the concept in his presidential address to the American Marketing Association n 1953.

5. Professor Frey dealt with the subject in a pamphlet entitled. "The Effective Marketing Mix," and published by the Amos Tuck School of Business Administration in 1956.

11

THE CONCEPT OF THE MARKETING MIX

A marketing mix is the unique combination of marketing procedures and policies used by a firm. The marketing mix evolves from the firm's strategy and tactics, its resources, and market forces. An optimizing marketing mix must blend empirical information with an assessment of future market empirical information with an assessment of future market trends, Understanding an application of the marketing mix is a step forward in the development of scientific marketing.

I have always found it interesting to observe how an apt or colourful term may catch on, gain wide usage, and help to further understanding of a concept that has already been expressed in less appealing and communicative terms Such a s been true of the phrase "marketing mix." Which I began to use in my teaching and writing some 15 years ago. In a relatively short time it has come to have wide usage. This not tells of the evolution of the marketing mix concept.

The phrase was suggested to me by a paragraph in a research bulletin on the management of marketing costs, written by my associate, Professor James Culliton (1948). In this study of manufacturers' marketing costs he described the business executive as a

"decider," and "artist"—a "mixer of ingredients," who

sometimes follows a recipe prepared by others, sometimes, prepares his own recipe as he goes along, sometimes adapts a recipe to the ingredients immediately available, and sometimes experiments with or invents ingredients no one else has tried.

I liked his idea of calling a marketing executive a "mixer of ingredients," one who is constantly engaged in fashioning creatively a mix of marketing procedures and policies in his efforts to produce a profitable enterprise.

For many years previous to Culliton's cost study the wide variation in the procedures and policies employed by managements of manufacturing firms in their marketing programmes and the correspondingly wide variation in the costs of these marketing functions, which Culliton aptly ascribed to the varied "mixed of ingredients," had become increasingly evident as we had gathered marketing cases at the Harard Business School. The marked differences in the patterns for formulae of the marketing programmes not only were evident through facts disclosed in case histories, but also were reflected clearly in the figures of a cost study of food manufacturers made by the Harvard bureau of Business Research in1929. The primary objective of this study was to determine common figures of expenses for various marketing functions among food manufacturing companies, similar to the common cost figures which had been determined in previous years for various kinds of retail and wholesale businesses. In this manufacturer's study we were unable, however, with the data gathered to determine common expense figures that had much significance as standards by which to guide management, such as had been possible in the studies of retail and wholesale trades, where the methods of operation tended toward uniformity. Instead, among food manufactures the ratios of sales devoted to the various functions of marketing such as advertising, personal selling, packaging, and so on, were found to be widely divergent, no matter how we grouped our respondents. Each respondent gave data that tended to uniquences.

Culliton's study of marketing costs in 1947—48 was a second effort to find out, among other objectives, whether a bigger sample and a more careful classification of companies would produce evidence of operating uniformities that would give helpful common expense figures. But the result was the same as in our early study: there was wide diversity in cost ratios among any classifications of firms which were set up, and no common figures were fond that had much value. This was true whether companies were grouped according to similarity in product lines, amount of sales, territorial extent of operations, or other bases of classification.

Relatively early in may study of advertising, it had become evident that understanding of advertising usage by manufacturers in any case had to come from an analysis of advertising's place as one element in the total marketing programme of the firm. I came to realize that it is essential always to ask: what overall marketing strategy has been or might e employed to bring about a profitable operation in light of the circumstances faced the management? What combination of marketing procedures and policies has been or might be adopted to bring about desired behaviour of trade and consumers at costs that will permit a profit? Specifically, how can advertising, personal selling, pricing, packaging, channels, warehouse and the other elements of a marketing programme be manipulated and fitted together in a way that will give a profitable operation? In short, I saw that every advertising management case called for a consideration of the strategy to be adopted for the total marketing programme, with advertising recognized as only one element whose form and extent depended on its careful adjustment to the other parts of the programme.

The soundness of this viewpoint was supported by case histories throughout my volume, *The Economic Effects f Advertising* (Borden, 1942). In the chapters devoted to the utilization of advertising by business, I had pointed out the innumerable combinations of marketing methods and policies that might be adopted by a manager in arriving at a marketing plan. For instance, in the area of branding, he might elect to marketing plan. For instance, in the area of branding, he might elect to adopt an individualized brand or a family brand. Or he might decide to sell his product branded or under private label. Any decision in the area of brand policy in turn has immediate implications that bear on his selection of channels of distribution, sales force methods, packaging, promotional procedure, and advertising. Throughout the volume the case materials cited show that the way in which any marketing function is designed and the burden placed upon the unction are determined largely by the overall marketing strategy adopted by managements to meet the market conditions under which they operate. The forces met by different firms vary widely. Accordingly, the programmes fashioned differ widely. Regarding advertising, which was the function under focus in the economic effects volume, I said at one point:

In all the above illustrative situations it should be recognized that advertising is not an operating method to be considered as something apart, as something whose profit value is to be judged alone. An able management does sẹt ask, "Shall we use of not use advertising," without consideration of the product and of other management procedures to be employed. Rather the question is always one of finding a management formula giving advertising is due place in the combination of manufacturing methods, product form, placing, promotion and selling methods, and distribution methods. As previously pointed out different formulate, i.e., different combinations of methods, say be profitably employed by competing manufacturers.

To portray this broadened concept in a visual presentation requires merely:

(1) a list of the important elements or ingredients that make up marketing programmes;

(2) a list of the forces that bear on the marketing operation of a firm and to which the marketing manager must adjust in his search for a mix of programme hat can be successful.

The list of elements of the marketing mix in such a visual presentation can be long or short, depending on how far one wishes to go in his classification and sub-classification of the marketing procedures and policies with which marketing managements deal when devising marketing programmes. The list of elements which I have employed in my teaching and consulting work covers the principal areas of marketing activities which call for management decisions as revealed by case histories. I realize other might build a different list. Mine is as follows:

Elements of the Marketing Mix of Manufacturers

1. Product Planning -policies and procedures relating to:
   - (a) Product lines to be offered—qualities, design, etc.
   - (b) Markets to sell: whom, where, when, and in what quantity,
   - (c) New product policy—research and development programme.
2. Pricing—policies and procedures relating to:
   - (a) Price level to adopt.
   - (b) Specific prices to adopt (odd-even, etc.).
   - (c) Price policy, e.g., one-price or varying price, price maintenance, list prices, etc.
3. Branding—policies and procedures relating to:
   - (a) Selection of trade marks.
   - (b) Brand policy—individualized or family brand.
   - (c) Sale under private label or unbranded.
4. Channels of Distribution—policies and procedures relating to:
   - (a) Channels to use between plant and consumer.
   - (b) Degree of selectivity among wholesalers and retailers.
   - (c) Efforts to gain cooperation of the trade.
5. Personal Selling—policies and procedures relating to:
   - (a) Burden to be placed on personal selling and the methods to be employed in:
     - (i) Manufacturer's organization.

(ii) Wholesale segment of the trade.

(iii) Retail segment of the trade.

6. Advertising—policies and procedures relating to:
   (a) Amount to spend—i.e., the burden to be placed on advertising
   (b) Copy platform to adopt:
      (i) Product image desired.
      (ii) Corporate image desired.
   (c) Mix of advertising: to the trade; through the trade; to consumers.
7. Promotions—policies and procedures relating to:
   (a) Burden to place on special selling plans or devices directed at or through the trade.
   (b) Form of these devices for consumer promotions, for trade promotions.
8. Packaging—policies and procedures relating to:
   (a) Formulation of package and label.
9. Display—polices and procedures relating to:
   (a) Burden to be put on display to help effect sale.
   (b) Methods to adopt to secure display.
10. Servicing—policies and procedures relating to:
    (a) Providing service needed.
11. Physical Handling—policies and procedures relating to:
    (a) Warehousing.
    (b) Transportation.
    (c) Inventories.
12. Fact Finding and Analysis—policies and procedures relating to:

(a) securing, analysis, and use of facts in marketing operations.

Also if one were to make a list of all the forces which managements weight at one time or another when formulating their marketing mixes, it would be very long indeed, for the behaviour of individuals and groups in all spheres of life have a bearing, first, on what goods and services are produced and consumed, and, second, on the procedures that may be employed in bringing about exchange of these goods and services. However, the important forces which bear on marketers, all arising from the behaviour of individuals or groups, may readily be listed under four heads timely the behaviour of consumers, the trade, competitors, and government.

The outline below contains these four behavioural forces with notations of some of the important behavioural determinants within each force. These must be studied and understood by the marketer, if his marketing it is to be successful. The great quest of marketing management is to understand the behaviour of humans in response to the stimuli to which they are subjected. The skillful marketer is one who is a perceptive and psychologist and sociologist, who has keen insight into individual and group behaviour, who can foresee changes in behaviour that develop a dynamic world, who has creative ability for building well-knit programmes because he has the capacity to visualize the probable response of consumers, trade, and competitors to his moves. His skill in forecasting response to his marketing moves should well be supplemented by a further skill in devising and using tests and measurements to check consumer trade response to his programme or parts thereof, for no marketer has so much prescience that he can proceed without empirical check.

Below, then, is the suggested outline of forces which govern the mixing of marketing elements. This list and that of the elements taken together provide a visual presentation of the concept of the marketing mix.

Market Forces bearing on the Marketing Mix

1. Consumers' Buying Behaviour, as determined by their:

(a) Motivation in purchasing.

(b) Buying habits.

(c) Living habits.

(d) Environment (present and future, as revealed by trends, for environment influences consumer's attitudes toward products and their use of them).

(e) Buying power.

(f) Number (i.e., how many).

2. The Trade's Behaviour – wholesalers' and retailers' behaviour, as influences by:

   (a) Their motivations

   (b) Their structure, practices, and attitudes.

   (c) Trends in structure, practices, and attitudes.

   (d) Trends in structure and procedures that portend change.

3. Competitor's Position and Behaviour, as influenced by:

   (a) Industry structure and the firm's relation thereto.

      (i) Size and strength of competitors.

      (ii) Number of competitors and degree of industry concentration.

      (iii) Indirect competition – i.e., from other products.

   (b) Relation of supply to demand – oversupply or undersupply.

   (c) Product choices offered consumers by the industry – i.e., quality price, service.

   (d) Degree to which competitors compete on price vs. non-price bases.

   (e) Competitors' motivations and attitudes – their likely response to actions of other firms.

   (f) Trends, technological and social portending changes in supply and demand.

4. Governmental Behaviour—Controls over marketing:
   (a) Regulations over products.
   (b) Regulations over pricing.
   (c) Regulations over competitive practices.
   (d) Regulations over advertising and promotion.

The manager must devise a mix of procedures that fit that resources. If his firm is small, he must judge the response of consumer trade, and competition in light of his position and resources and the influence that he can exert in the market. He must look for special opportunities in product or method of operation. The small firm cannot employ the procedures of the big firm. Though he may sell the same kind of product as the big firms, his marketing strategy is likely to be widely different in many respects. Innumerable instances of this fact might be cited. For example, in the industrial goods field, small firms often seek to build sales on a limited and highly specialized line, whereas industry leaders seek patronage for full lines. Small firms often elect to go in for regional sales rather than attempt the national distribution practiced by larger companies. Again, the company of limited resource often elects to limit its production and sales to products whose potentials too small to attract the big fellows. Still again, companies with small resources in the cosmetic field not infrequently have set up introductory marketing programmes employing aggressive personal selling and a "push" strategy with distribution limited to leading department stores. Their initially small advertising funds have been directed through these selected retail outlets, with the offering of the products and their story told over the signatures of the stores. The strategy has been to borrow kudos for their products from the leading stores reputations and to gain a gradual radiation of distribution to smaller stores in all types of channels, such as often comes from the trade's follow-the leader behaviour. Only after resources have grown from mounting sales has a dense retail distribution been aggressively sought and a shift made to place the selling burden more and more on company-signed advertising.

The above strategy was employed for Toni products and

Stoppette deodorant in their early marketing stages when the resources of their producers were limited (cf. case of Jules Montenier, Inc. In Borden and Marshall, 1959, pp 498-518). In contrast, cosmetic manufacturers with large resources have generally followed a "pull" strategy for the introduction of new products, relying on heavy campaigns of advertising in a rapid succession of a are introductions to induce a hoped-for, complete retail coverage from the start (cf. case of Bristol-Myers Company in Borden and Marshall, 1959, pp. 519-533). These introductory campaigns have been undertaken only after careful programmes of product development and test marketing have given assurance that product and selling plans had high promise of success.

Long Versus Short Term aspects of Marketing Mix

There are continuous tactical maneuvers: a new product, aggressive promotion, or price change initiated by a competitor must be considered and met; the failure of the trade to provide adequate market coverage or display must be remedied; a faltering sales force must be reorganized an stimulated; a decline in sales has are must be diagnosed and remedied; an advertising approach that has lost effectiveness must be replaced; a general business decline must countered. All such problems call for a management's maintaining effective channels of information relative to its own operations and to the day-to-day behaviour of consumers, competitors, and the trade. Thus, we ma observe that short range forces play a large part in the fashioning of the mix to be used at anytime and in determining the allocation of expenditures among the various functional accounts of the operating statement.

But the overall strategy employed in a marketing mix is the product of longer range plans and procedures dictated in part by past empiricism and in part, if the management is a good one, by management foresight as to what needs to be done to keep the form successful in a changing world. As the world has become more and more dynamic, blessed is that corporation which has managers who have foresight, who can study trends of all kinds – natural, economic, social, and technological – and, guided by these, devise long-range plans than give promise of keeping their corporations afloat and successful in the turbulent sea of market change. Accordingly, when we think of the marketing mix, we need to give particular heed today to devising a mix based on long-range planning that promises to fit the world of five or ten or more years hence. Provision for effective long-range planning in corporate organization and procedure has become more and more recognized as the earmark of good management in a world that has become increasing subject to rapid change.

To cite an instance among American marketing organizations which has shown foresight in adjusting the marketing mix to meet social and economic change, I look upon Sears Roebuck and Company as an outstanding example. After building an unusually successful mail order businesses to meet the needs of a rural America, sears management foresaw the need to depart from its marketing pattern as a mail order company catering Primarily to farmers. The trend from a rural to an urban United States was going on apace. The automobile and good roads promised to make town and city stores increasingly available to those who continued to be farmers. Relatively early, Sears launched a chain of stores across the land, each easily accessible by highway to both farmer and city resident and with adequate parking space for customers. In time there followed the remarkable telephone and mail order plan directed at urban resident to make buying easy for Americans when congested city streets and highways made shopping increasingly distasteful. Similarly, in the areas of planning products which would meet the desires of consumers in a fast changing world, of shapping its servicing to meet the needs of a wide variety of mechanical products, of pricing procedures to meet the challenging competition that came with the advent of discount retailers, the Sears organization has shown a foresight, adaptability, and creative ability worthy of emulation. The amazing growth and profitability of the company attest to the foresight and skill o its management. Its history shows the wisdom of careful attention to market forces and their impending change in devising marketing mixes that may assure growth.

Use of the Marketing Mix Concept

Like many concepts, the marketing mix concept seems relatively simple, once it has been expressed. I know that before they were ever tagged with the nomenclature of "concept," the ideas involved were widely understood among marketers as a result of the growing knowledge about marketing and marketing procedures that came during the preceding half century. But I have found for myself that once the ideas were reduced to a formal statement with an accompanying visual presentation, the concept of the mix has proved a helpful device in teaching, in business problem solving, and, generally, as an aid to thinking about marketing. First of all, it is helpful in giving an answer to the question often raised as to "what is marketing?" A chart which shows the elements of the mix and the forces that bear on the mix helps to bring understanding of what marketing is. It helps to explain why in our dynamic world the thinking of management in all its functional areas must be oriented to the market.

In recent years I have kept an abbreviated chart showing the elements and the forces of the marketing mix in front of my classes at all times. In case discussion it has proved a handy device by which to raise queries as to whether the student has recognized the implications of any recommendation the might have made in the areas of the several elements of the mix. Or, referring to the forces, we can question whether all the pertinent market forces have been given due consideration. Continual reference to the mix chart leads me to feel that the students' understanding of "what marketing is" is strengthened. The constant presence and use of the chart leaves a deeper understanding that marketing is the devising of programmes that successfully meet the forces of the market.

In problem solving the marketing mix chart is a constant reminder of:

(i) The fact that a problem seemingly lying in one segment of the mix must be deliberated with constant thought regarding the effect of any change is that sector on the other areas of marketing operations.

(ii) The need of careful study of the market forces as they might bear on problems in hand.

In short, the mix chart provides an ever ready checklist as to areas into which to guide thinking when considering marketing questions or dealing with marketing problems.

Marketing: Science or Art?

The quest for a "science of marketing" is hard upon us. If science is in part a systematic formulation and arrangement of facts in a way to help understanding, then the concept of the marketing mix may possibly be considered a small contribution in the search for a science of marketing. If we think of a marketing science as involving the observation and classification of facts and the establishment of verifiable laws that can be used by the marketer as a guide to action with assurance that predicted results will ensue, then we cannot be said to have gotten far toward establishing a science. The concept of the mix layout the areas in which facts should be assembled, these to serve as a guide to management judgement in building marketing mixes. In the last few decades. American marketers have made substantial progress in adopting the scientific method in assembling facts. They have sharpened the tools of fact finding—both those arising within the business and those external to it. Aided by these fact and by the skills developed through careful observation and experience, markets are better fitted to practice the art of designing marketing mixes than would be the case had not the techniques of gathering facts been advance d as they have been in recent decades. Moreover, marketers have made progress in the use of the scientific method in designing tests whereby the results from mixes or parts of mixes can be measured. Thereby marketers have been learning how to subject the hypotheses of their mix artists to empirical check.

With continued improvement in the search for and the recording of facts pertinent to marketing, with further application of the controlled experiment, and with an extension and careful recording of case histories we may hope for a gradual formulation of clearly defined and helpful marketing laws. Until then, and even then, marketing and the building of marketing mixes will largely lie in the realm of art.

REFERENCES

Borden, Neil H. *The Economic Effects of Advertising*. Homewood, Ill.: Richard D. Irwin, 1942.

Borden, Neil H., And M.V. Marshall. *Advertising Management: Text and Cases*. Homewood, Ill.: Richard D. Irwin, 1959

Culliton, James W. *The Management of Marketing Costs*. Boston: Division of Research, Graduate School of Business Administration, Harvard University, 1948.

12

PRICE ELASTICITY TO THE MARKETING MIX—AND BEYOND

The achievement of corporate marketing objectives depends on customer response to the firm's marketing mix. Demand, demand elasticity, and the marketing mix are critical elements in the firm's efforts to reach marketing objectives. "Customer appeals mix" describes customer perception of the total satisfaction associated with a particular offering of the firm. There is a significant difference between the customer appeals mix concept and the marketing mix concept. A marketing programme is a synthesis of marketing mix concept. A marketing programme is a synthesis of marketing mix elements created to influence the customer-appeals mix.

Marketing executives are concerned, perhaps, beyond all else, with customers' responses to their sales efforts. This paper accordingly traces the development of that stream of ideas which relates to demand – that is, to the effects of sellers' actions upon customer behaviour. It Starts with the demand curve and the related concept of demand elasticity and then discusses the marketing mix concept. Thereupon, it introduces two somewhat new notions; "marketing programmes" and "the customer appeals mix," These notions are designed mainly to eliminate ambiguities in the marketing mix concept.

The Demand Curve and Price Elasticity

As developed by classical and neo-classical economists, eh demand curve summarizes all that a price-setter needs to know about the customers. It indicates how many units they would buy at different prices. Properly constructed, it would take account of the following factors: (1) customer's responses; (2) competitors' responses; (3) the effects of reaching a given price by an increase as opposed to reaching that price by a decrease (this point related to the reversibility of the demand curve). In addition, the demand curve "takes account of" other sales devices than price by holding them constant. (No account is taken, it should be noted of the possibility that the slope of a demand curve might differ markedly according to the amount of other sales devices that are held constant).

Neoclassical theorists developed the concept of price elasticity of demand, to describe variations in the sensitivity of unit sales to changes in price. One can describe, by an elasticity measure, the response of customers as a whole to varying price changes. (Here again, economists simplified matters a good but by assuming that customers' responses would be much the same at all levels of price).

With the writings of Edward Chamberlin, one other sales device was considered explicitly in demand theory. Specifically, promotional efforts were discussed frontally, and the concept of "promotional elasticity of demand" made its appearance. No much later, the concept of income elasticity of demand was formulated. Demand theory at the present time largely revolves about there determinants of unit sales; price, promotional outlays and level of national income.

The Marketing Mix Concept

Marketing specialists have pushed ahead in a different direction since World War II. Their contributions started in 1947 when Professor Neil Borden coined the phrase "marketing mix." Although as originally stated, this concept was simply a long list of the marketing activities in which many businesses engage in order to win customers, the "marketing mix" became the focal point of a significant extension of demand theory. The greatest single advance can be credited to the very interesting article published by Professor P.J. Verdoorn early in1956. He established the parallel between the marketing mix and production theory. (He made other contributions as well, especially by placing the concept of the marketing mix—as he came to use it—within the structure of decision theory).

The marketing mix concept makes explicit the fact that top management consciously or unconsciously allocates resources among alternative and partially-substitute marketing activities. One consequence is the recognition that a firm would gain by bringing together under a single intelligence all of the activities that relate to the customer—the main organizational result of the "new marketing conçept." Also, the marketing mix concept provided "room" for any and all marketing activities and broke the bounds that limited discussion of sales determinants to price promotion and income.

The marketing mix concept has fairly grave limitations, however. Even in 1965, as one examines it closely, he finds very great fuzziness. The measurement of an company's marketing mix poses very great difficulties which will only be intimated here. First, it does not explain what proportion of product costs should be charged to marketing—or how to drawn line between say, packaging and delivery costs that are marketing and those that are non-marketing costs. Second, it does not show how one might assign a cost to price—which clearly is one and a major element of the marketing mix. This factor involves no direct monetary outlay and must, somehow, be measured indirectly. Third, it fails to relate a firm's marketing efforts to specific types of customers. Clearly, a firm can select among alternative marketing programmes only if it is conscious of the kinds of customers to whom it is trying to appeal, Fourth, it calls for horrendous efforts if one is to measure or estimate the payoff of alternative mardous efforts if one is to measure or estimate the payoff of alternative marketing efforts.

Perhaps the greatest fuzziness in the marketing mix concept results from the shifting perspectives that it invites. As usually interpreted, the marketing mix denotes a fir's total expenditures for marketing and the proportions of that total that are devoted to different uses. The term also is used sometimes to refer to the way that customers are affected by these expenditures. That is, advertising expenditures are taken to be directly related to the strength of a company's advertising appeals; a firm's "outlays" for products are taken to be proportional to the product appeal that customers receive. In other words, most writings imply a direct equivalence between marketing outlays on one hand and the benefits or attractions offered to customers on the other.

A little reflection shows that thee need be no direct connection between a firm's outlays and its customers' perceptions of that firm's offerings. In the first place, the attractions that customers perceive in a firms' offering at any time more often reflect its past expenditures than those of the present. A firm's reputation and the other intangible values inhering in its brand name oftener mainly a residue of past advertising and past customer experience with that brand; current advertising expenditures may contribute relatively little. Conversely, some heavy advertisers still are perceived to offer negative intangible values because of past product failures or a poor service record.

In the second place, marketing efforts vary widely in their perceptual impact. One firm's expenditures of one million dollars on advertising might do far more to create customer readiness to buy than a similar expenditure by its competitors. Indeed, the same company might get far more customer impact from a given expenditure now than from the same outlay last year.

Third, some marketing outlays by firms are not intended to create a customer appeal. Included among such outlays are purchases of equipment for handling, storage and delivery of product; the outlays required to open up new territories; the cost of adding and dropping distributors, etc. Instead, their purpose may be to reduce future marketing costs or to expand the scope of the firm's efforts. Since marketing outlays are to correlated closely with customer's perceptions, another concept is clearly needed. This concept, termed the "customer appeals mix." Means what the words imply; it denotes the benefits that the firm's target customers perceive in the firms total offering. Rather than being measure in dollars spent by the firm, it is measured b its target customers' perceptions of the firm's offering. Obviously, individual customers' perceptions of the benefits offered by any and will vary. Usually a firm benefits from grouping prospective customers into customer "types' or segments, each of which is fairly similar in the benefits perceived and desired in the product.

"Customer Appeals Mix"

This concept possesses several difficulties, even if it satisfies an obvious need. First, one must expect substantial differences in customer's perceptions of any offerings; therefore, one must find a way of describing "the customer appeal mixes. Second, one must find some technique by which one can describe these appeals accurately and quantitatively. Third, one must develop a method of identifying customer appeals in a way that is lacking at present. Since the first two points are self-evident, though extremely difficult, we shall confine our attention to the third. The marketing mix is generally broken down into such things as price advertising, personal selling, product, customer service, marketing research, distributor development and the like. Customer appeals, on the other than, are best described in very different terms and doubtless vary widely from product to product. Among the more obvious customer appeals are the following: convenience in purchase, convenience in the use of the product, distinctiveness, a "feeling of luxury," reliability confidence, freedom from interrupted usage, speedy repair and the like.

Two points follow from the foregoing list; first, the terms used to define the marketing mix do not rapidly apply to the elements in the customer appeals mix. Second, and more important, a combination to marketing mix elements usually is required to create a particular customer appeal. For example, a firm may redesign its product, change its package carry out certain types of a advertising, indoctrinate retail salesmen, etc., order to convey a customer appeal of luxuriousness. This example illustrates that four marketing mix elements can be combined effectively to create one customer appeal.

Important consequences follow from this as conclusion: namely marketing expenditures probably should not be regarded as marketing mix components. More specifically, a marketing executive might be unwise to conceptualize his outlays in terms of price, advertising, personal sales etc. Instead, he might conceptualize them in them in terms of the customer appeals that they are intended to create. He will try to put together in a single package—which we shall call a "marketing programme"—all of the elements than combine to create customer appeals by the most efficient methods available to him.

The Marketing Programme

As indicated, many firms do not think of marketing efforts as consisting of isolated activities like pricing, advertising, etc. Instead, they fashion what we call "marketing programmes" which represent a bundle of marketing efforts which have an explicit goal. That goal usually is to create a particular customer appeal; though it could aim to reduce marketing costs also.

The chief distinguishing features of marketing programmes are; First, they have explicit objectives—are not designed simply to raise profits. Second, they consist of the combination of marketing expenditures rather tan a single one. These fit together, ordinarily in a manner that reinforces the effects of each one. Third, marketing programmes, unlike elements in the marketing mix, are also distinguished their originality and uniqueness. One does not simply vary the proportions of different types of marketing efforts to find that combination which gives greatest total impact. Rather, one conceives of a particular approach—possibly a unique customer appeal—and then puts together the measures that will bring it into existence.

The relationship among the chief concepts discussed here is perhaps best expressed in a few simple statements:

1. Firms' marketing efforts are designed to achieve a hierarchy of business objectives. Two key intervening objectives

are; (1) Target customer segments; and (2) A customer appeals mix.

2. In developing and selecting among alternative marketing actions, marketing managers should start with a description of their existing customer appeals mix – that is, they should know how potential target customers perceive their offerings.

3. They will want to develop a bundle of marketing programmes that would them closer to their "target customer appeals mix" – taking account of relative cost and effectiveness of their alternatives. The target customer appeals mix is the one that management seeks to establish and may be very different from the one that prevails.

4. The marketing expenditures that result from these marketing programmes may be described as the firm's marketing mix. A marketing mix largely reflects a firm's efforts to move from its current customer appeals mix to as target customer appeals mix.

Summary and Conclusions

This article sketches the development of ideas that deal with customers' reactions to measures taken by businesses to sell their products. It shows that economic theory contributes the demand curve which, with embellishments, develops into the price, promotional and income elasticities of demand. It further reviews the marketing specialists' contributions and finds that they take the form of the marketing mix concept.

An analysis of the marketing mix shows it to be deficient on several scores. To rectify these deficiencies and to supplement it, two additional notions are set forth: the customer appeals mix and the marketing programme. Both of these notions have a conceptual vale in themselves. More over, they sharpen ideas that are only set forth in a hazy manner in the market mix concept.

13

CONSUMER BEHAVIOUR ANALYSIS

Introduction

All activities of the business must be focused on the consumer. This is an essential viewpoint in forms that operate under the marketing management concept. Any business unable to provide goods and services that fulfill the needs and satisfy the wants of consumers has lost its prime reasons for existence; it will not long survive in a competitive environment. Consumers judge business performance and determine business destinies by the manner in which they, consumers, exercise their purchasing power. Thus, whether a business is rewarded or penalized in the market-place is determined to a large extent by how well the needs and wants of its customers are understood and fulfilled.

Consumer reactions to market offerings result from a myriad of influences. Marketing managers must endeavour to understand the complexities of consumer behaviour and give due weight to what they believe to be the more important forces acting on the consumer. Before marketing opportunities can be recognized and marketing strategies adapted customer traits or characteristics that permit target market identification or segmentation must be studied. Selections in this chapter were chosen for their potential contribution to an understanding and appreciation of consumer behaviour and the forces underlying that behaviour.

Changing life styles for consumption and spending units have introduced important consideration for managers who must evaluate marketing opportunities. Discretionary time, mobility, and purchasing power helped to create a more discerning customer who in purchase decision may assign greater significance to convenience costs than to commodity cost. Similarly, social class and demographic methods of market segmentation , although still important, need to be combined with newer tools of marketing analysis. The satisfaction of customers and the attainment of marketing objectives results from successful integration of these elements.

Governmental agencies and other distinctive groups constitute specious markets that present unique marketing problems and opportunities. These markets must be analyzed in dept if their potentials are to be capitalized.

Sound marketing decisions are based on a knowledge of consumer motivations. Man is characterized as a wanting animal with a hierarchy of needs. Behaviour should be looked at a channel through which multiple needs are expressed and satisfied.

A Theory of Human Motivation

In a previous chapters various propositions were presented which would have to be included in any theory of human motivation that could lay claim to being definitive. These conclusions may be briefly summarized as follows:

1. The integrated wholeness of the organism must be one of the foundation stones of motivation theory.
2. The hunger drive (or any other physiological drive) was rejected as a centering point or model for a definitive theory of motivation. Any drive that is somatically based and localizable was shown to be atypical rather than typical in human motivation.
3. Such a theory should stress and center itself upon ultimate or basic goals rather than partial or superficial ones, upon ends rather than means to these ends. Such a stress would

imply a more central place for unconscious than for conscious motivations.

4. There are usually available various cultural paths to the same goal. Therefore, conscious, specific, local-cultural desires are not as fundamental in motivation theory as the more basic, unconscious goals.
5. Any motivated behavior, either preparatory or consummatory, must be understood to be a channel through which many basic needs may be simultaneously expressed or satisfied. Typically an act has more than one motivation.
6. Practically all organismic states are to be understood as motivated and as motivating.
7. Human needs arrange themselves in hierarchies of prepotency. That is to say, the appearance of one need usually rests on the prior satisfaction of another, more prepotent need. Man is a perpetually wanting animal. Also no need or drive can be treated as if it were isolated or discrete; every drive is related to the state of satisfaction or dissatisfaction of other drives.
8. Lists of drives will get us nowhere for various theoretical and practical reasons. Furthermore, any classification of motivations must deal with the problem of levels of specificity or generalization of the motives to be classified.
9. Classifications of motivation must be based upon goals rather than upon instigating drives or motivated behaviour.
10. Motivation theory should be human-centered rather than animal-centered.
11. The situation or the field in which the organism reacts must be taken into account, but the field itself must be interpreted in terms of the organism. Field theory cannot be a substitute for motivation theory.
12. Not only the integration of the organism must be taken into account, but also the possibility of isolated, specific, partial or segmental reactions.

It has since become necessary to add to these another affirmation.

13. Motivation theory is not synonymous with behaviour theory. The motivations are only one class of determinants of behaviour. While behaviour is almost always motivated, it is also almost always biologically, culturally and situationally determined as well...

Summary

There are at least five set of goals, which we may call basic needs. These are briefly physiological, safety, love, esteem, and self-actualization various conditions upon which these basic satisfactions rest and by certain more intellectual desires.

These basic goals are related to each other, being arranged in a hierarchy of prepotency. This means that the most prepotent goal will monopolize consciousness and will tend of itself to organize the recruitment of the various capacities of the organism. The less prepotent needs are minimized, even forgotten or denied. But when a need is fairly well satisfied, the next prepotent ("higher") need emerges, in turn to dominate the conscious life and to serve as the center of organization of behaviour, since gratified needs are not active motivators.

Thus man is a perpetually wanting animal. Ordinarily the satisfaction of these wants is not altogether mutually exclusive, but only tends to be. The average member of our society is most often partially satisfied and partially unsatisfied in all of his wants. The hierarchy principle is usually empirically observed in terms of increasing percentages of non-satisfaction as we go up the hierarchy. Reversals often average order of the hierarchy are sometimes observed. Also it has been observed that an individual may permanently lose the higher wants in the hierarchy under special conditions. There are not only ordinarily multiple motivations for usual behaviour, but in addition many determinants other than motives.

Any thwarting or possibility of thwarting of these basic human goals, or danger to the defenses which protect them, or to the conditions upon which they rest, is considered to be a psychological thereat. With a few exceptions, all psychopathology may be partially traced to such threats. A basically thwarted man may actually be defined as a "sick" man, if we wish.

It is such basic threats which bring about the general emergency reactions.

Certain other basic problems have not been dealt with because of limitations of space. Among these are (a) the problem of values in any definitive motivation theory, (b) the relation between appetites, desires, needs and hat is "good" for the organism, (c) the etiology of the basic needs and their possible derivation in early childhood, (d) redefinition of motivational concepts, i.e., drive, desire, wish, need, goal, (e) implication of our theory for hedonistic theory. (f) the nature of the uncompleted act, of success and failure, and of aspiration-level , (g) the role of association, habit and conditioning, (h) relation to the theory of interpersonal relations, (i) implications for psychotherapy, (j) implication for theory of society, (k) the theory of selfishness (l) the relation between needs and cultural patterns, (m) the relation between this theory and All port's theory of functional autonomy. These as well as certain other less important questions must be considered as motivation theory attempts to become definitive.

Behavioural Models for Analyzing Buyers

Marketing decisions are based upon assumptions concerning consumer behaviour. A consumer's overt purchasing behaviour is a function of several factors, all processed by his psyche. Five "partial" behavioural models are presented, and their underlying theories are evaluated.

In times past, management could arrive at a fair understanding of its buyers through the daily experience of selling to them. But the growth is the size of firms and markets has removed many decision-makers from direct contact with buyers. Increasingly, decision-makers have had to turn to summary statistics and to behavioural theory, and are spending most money today than ever before to try to understand their buyers.

Who buys? How do they buy? And why? The first two questions relate to relatively overt aspects of buyer behaviour, and can be learned about through direct observation and interviewing.

But uncovering why people buy is a extremely difficult task. The answer will tend to vary with the investigator's behavioural frame of reference.

The buyer is subject to many influences which trace a complex country throughhis psyche and lead eventually to overt purchasing responses. This conception of the buying process is illustrated in Figure 1. Various influences and theirmodes of transmission are shown at the left. At the right are the buyer's responses in choiceof prodct, brand, dealer, quantities,and frequency. In the center stands the buyer and his mysterious psychological processes. The buyer's psyche is a "black box" who workings can be only partially deduced. The marketing strategist's challenge to the beavioural scientist is to construct a more specific model of the mechanism in the black box.

Unfortunately no generally accepted model of the mechanism exist. The human mind, the only entity in nature with deep powers of understanding, still remains the least understood. Scientists can explain planetary motion, genetic determination, and molecular behaviour. Yet they have only partial, and often partisan, models, of human behaviour.

Nevertheless, the marketing strategist should recognize the potential interpretative contributions of different partial models for explaining buyer behaviour. Depending upon the product, different variables and behavioural mechanisms may assume particular importance. A psychoanalytic behavioural model might throw much light on the factors operating in cigarette demand, while an economic behavioural model might be useful in explaining machine-tool purchasing. Sometimes alternative models may shed light on different demand aspects of the same product.

What are the most useful behavioural models for interpreting the transformation of buying influences into purchasing responses? Five different models of the buyer's "black box" are presented in the present article, along with their respective marketing applications: (1) the Marshallian model stressing economic motivations; (2) the Pavlovian model, learning; (3) the Freudian model, psychoanalytic motivations; (4) the Veblenian model, social-psychological factors; and (5) the Hobbesian model, organizational factors. These models represent radically different conceptions of the mainsprings of human behaviour.

The Marshallian Economic Model

Economists were the first professional group to construct a specific theory of buyer behaviour. The theory holds that purchasing decisions are the result of largely "rational" and conscious economic calculations. The individual buyer seeks to spend his income on those goods that will delivery the most utility (satisfaction) according to his tastes and relative prices.

The antecedents for this view trace back to the writings of Adam Smith and Jeremy Bentham. Smith set the tone by developing a doctrine of economic growth based on the principle that man is motivated by self-interest in all his actions. Bentham refined this view and saw man as finely calculating and weighting he expected pleasures and pains of every contemplated action.

Bentham's "felicific calculus" was not applied to consumer behaviour (as opposed to entrepreneurial behaviour) until the late 19th century. Then the "marginal-utility" theory of value was formulated independently and almost simultaneously by Jevons and Marshall in England, Menger in Austria, and Walras in Switzerland.

Alfred Marshal was the great consolidator of the classical and neoclassical tradition in economics; and his synthesis in the form of demand supply analysis constitutes the main source of modern micro-economic thought in the English-speaking world. His theoretical work aimed at realism, but his method was to start with simplifying assumptions and to examine the effect of a change in a single variable (say, price) when all other variables were held constant.

He would "reason out" the consequences of the provisional

assumptions and in subsequent steps modify his assumptions in direction of more realism. He employed the "measuring rod of money" as an indicator of the intensity of human psychological desires. Over the years his methods and assumptions have been refined into what is now known as modern utility theory: economic man is bent on maximizing his utility, and does this by carefully calculating the "felicific" consequences of any purchase...

Marketing Applications of Marshallian Model

From one point of view the Marshallian model is tautological and therefore neither true nor false. The model holds that they buyer acts in the light of his best "interest." But this is not very informative.

A second view is that this is a normative rather than a descriptive model of behaviour. The model provides logical norms for buyers who want to be "rational". Although the consumer is not likely to employ economic analysis to decide between a box of Kleenex and Scotties, he may apply economic analysis in deciding whether to buy anew car. Industrial buyers even more clearly would want an economic calculus for making good decisions.

A third view is that economic factors operate to a greater or lesser extent in all markets, and, therefore, must be included in any comprehensive description of buyer behaviour.

Furthermore, the model suggests useful behavioural hypotheses such as: (a) The lower the price of the product, the higher the sales. (b) The lower the price of substitute products, the lower the sales of this product; and the lower the price of complementary products, the higher the sales of this product. (c) The higher the real income, the higher the sales of this product, provided that it is not an "unferior" good. (d) The higher the promotional expenditures, the higher the sales.

The validity of these hypotheses does not rest on whether all individuals act as economic calculating machines in making their purchasing decisions. For example, some individuals may buy less of a product when its price is reduced. They may think that the quality has gone down, or that ownership has less status value. If a majority of buyers view price reductions negatively, ten sales may fall, contrary to the first hypothesis.

But for most goods a price reduction increases the relative value of the goods in many buyers' minds and leads to increased sales. This and the other hypotheses are intended to describe average effects.

The impact of economic factors in actual buying situations is studied through experimental design or statistical analyses of past data. Demand equations have been fitted to a wide variety of products – including beer, refrigerators, and chemical fertilizers. More recently, the impact of economic variables on the fortunes of different brands has been pursued with significant results, particularly in the case of coffee, frozen orange juice, and margarine.

But economic factors alone cannot explain all the variations in sales. The Marshallian model ignores the fundamental question of how product and brand preferences are formed. It represents a useful frame of reference for analyzing only one small corner of the "black box."

The Pavlovian Learning Model

The designation of a Pavlovian learning model ha sits origin in the experiments of the Russian psycholoist Pavlov, who range a bell each time before feeding a god. Soon he was able to induce the dog to salivate by ringing the bell whether or not food was supplied. Pavlov concluded that learning was largely an associative process and that a large component of behaviour was conditioned in this way...

The model has been refined over the year, and today is based on four central concepts – those of drive, cue, response, and reinforcement.

Drive. Also called needs or motives, drive refers to strong stimuli internal to the individual which impels action. Psychologists draw a distinction between primary physiological drives – such as hunger, thirst cold, pain, and sex – and learned drives which are derived socially – such as cooperation, fear, and acquisitiveness.

Cue. A drive is very general and impels a particular response only in relation to a particular configuration of cues. Cues are weaker stimuli in the environment and/or in the individual which determine when, where and how the subject responds...

Response. The response is he organism's reaction to the configuration of cues. Yet the same configuration of cues will not necessarily product the same response in the individual. This depends on the degree to which the experience was rewarding, that is, drive-reducing.

Reinforcement. If the experience is rewarding, a particular response is reinforced; that is, it is strengthened and there is a tendency for it to be repeated when the same configuration of cues appears again...

Forgetting, in contrast to extinction, is the tendency for learned associations to weaker, not because of the lack of reinforcement but because of nonuse.

Cue configurations are constantly changing. The housewife sees a new brand of coffee next to her habitual brand, or notes a special price deal on a rival brand. Experimental psychologists have found that the same learned response will be elicited similar patterns of cues; that is, leaned responses are generalized...

A counter-tendency to generalization is discrimination. When a housewife tries two similar brands and finds one more rewarding, her ability to discriminate between similar cue configurations improves. Discrimination increases the specificity of the cue-response connection, while generalization decrease the specificity.

The Freudian Psychoanalytic Model

The Freudian model of man is well known, so profound has benefits impact on 20th century thought. It is the latest of a series of philosophical "blows' to which man has been exposed in the last 500 years...

According to freud, the child enters the world driven by instinctual needs which he cannot gratify by himself. Very quickly and painfully he realizes his separateness from the rest of the world and yet his dependence on it.

He tries to get others to gratify his needs through a variety of blatant means, including intimidation and supplication. Continual frustration leads him to perfect more subtle mechanisms for gratifying his instincts.

As he grows, his psyche becomes increasingly complex. A part of his psyche—the id—remains the reservoir of his strong drives and urges. Another part—the ego—becomes his conscious planning center for finding outlets for his drives. And a third part—his super-ego—channels his instinctive drives into socially approved outlets to avoid the pain of guilt or shame.

The guilt or shame which man feels toward some of his urges—especially his sexual urges—causes him to repress them form his consciousness. Through such defense mechanisms as rationalisation and sublimation, these urges are denied or become transmuted into socially approved expressions. Yet these urges are never eliminated or under perfect control...

The individual's behaviour, therefore, is never simple. His motivational wellsprings are to obvious to a casual observer nor deeply understood by the individual himself. If he is asked why he purchased an expensive foreign sports-car, he may replay that he likes its maneuverability and its looks. At a deeper level he may have purchased the car to impress others or to feel young again. At a still deeper level, he may be purchasing the sports-car to achieve substitute gratification for unsatisfied sexual strivings.

Many refinement and changes in emphasis have occurred in this model since the time of Freud. This instinct concept has been replaced by a more careful delineation of basic drives; the three parts of the psyche are regarded now as theoretical concepts rather than actual entities; and the behavioural perspective has been extended to include cultural as well as biological mechanisms...

Marketing Applications of Freudian Model

Perhaps the most important marketing implication of this model is that buyers are motivated by symbolic as well as economic-functional product concerns. The change of a bar of soap from a square to a round shape may be more important in its sexual than its functional connotations. A cake mix that is advertised as involving practically no labour may alienate housewives because the easy life may evoke a sense of guilt.

Motivational research has produced some interesting and occasionally some bizarre hypotheses about what may been the buyer's mind regarding certain purchases. Thus, it has been suggested at one time or another that. Many businessman doesn't fly because of a fear of posthumous guilt—if he crashed, his wife would think of him as stupid for not taking a train.

Men want their cigars to be odoriferous, in order to prove that they (the men) are masculine.

A woman is very serious when she bakes a cake because unconsciously she is going through the symbolic act of given birth.

A man buys a convertible as a substitute "mistress."

Consumer prefer vegetable shortening because animal fats stimulate a sense of sin.

Men who wear suspenders are reacting to an unresolved castration complex.

There are admitted difficulties of providing these assertions Two prominent motivational researchers. Ernest Dichter and James Vicary, were employed independently b two separate groups in the prune industry to determine why so many people dislike prunes. Dichter found, among other things, that the prune aroused feelings of old age and insecurity in people, whereas Vicary's main finding was that Americans had an emotional block about prunes' laxative qualities. Which is the more valid interpretation? Or if they are both operative, which motive is found with greater statistical frequency in the population?

Unfortunately the usually survey techniques—direct observation and interviewing—can be used to establish the representatives of more superficial characteristics—age and family size, for example—but are not feasible for establishing the frequency of mental states which are presume dot be deeply "buried" within each individual.

Motivational researchers have to employ time-consuming projective techniques in the hope of throwing individual "egos" off guard, when carefully administered and interpreted techniques such as word association, sentence completion, picture interpretation, and role-playing can provide some insights into the minds of the small groups of examined individuals; but a "lea of faith" is sometimes necessary to generalize these findings to the population.

Nevertheless, motivation research can lead to useful insights and provide inspiration to creative men in he advertising and packaging world. Appeals aimed at the buyer's private world of hopes, dreams, and fears can often be as effective in stimulating purchase as more rationally-directed appeals.

The Veblenian Social-Psychological Model

While most economists have been content to interpret buyer behaviour is Marshallian terms, Thorstein Veblen struck out in different directions.

Veblen was trained as an ortfiodox economist, but evolved into a social thinker greatly influenced by the new science of social anthropology. He saw man as primarily a *social animal*—conforming to the general forms and norms of his larger culture and to the more specific standards of the subcultures and face-to-face groupings to which his life is bound. His wants and behaviour are largely molded by his present group-memberships and his aspired group-memberships.

Veblen's best-known example of this is in his description of the leisurt class. His hypothesis is that much of economic consumption is motivated not by intrinsic needs or satisfaction so much as by prestige-seeking. He emphasized the strong emulative factors operating in the choice of conspicuous goods like clothes, cars, and houses.

Some of his points, however, seem overstated by today's perspective. The leisure class does not serve as everyone's reference group; many persons aspire to the social patterns of the class immediately above it. And important segments of the affluent class practice conspicuous underconsumption rather than overconsumption. There are many people in all classes who are more anxious to "fit in" than to "stand out." As an example, William H. Whyte found that many families avoided buying air conditioners and other appliances before their neighbours did.

Marketing Applications of Veblenian Model

The various streams of thought crystallized into the modern social sciences of sociology, cultural anthropology and social psychology. Basic to them is the view that mans attitudes and behaviour are influenced by several levels of society—culture, subcultures, social classes, references groups, and face-to-face groups. The challenge to the marketer is to determine which of these social levels are the most important in influencing the demand for his product.

Culture

The most enduring influences are from culture. Man tends to assimilies his culture's mores and folkways, and to believe in their absolute rightner until deviants appear within his culture or until he confronts members of another culture.

A culture tends to lose its homogeneity as its population increased. When people no longer are able to maintain face-to-face relationships another culture.

Subcultures

A culture tends to lose its homogeneity as its population increaser. When people no longer are able to maintain face-to-face relationship with more than a small proportion of other members of a culture, smaller units or subcultures develop, which help to satisfy the individual's needs for more specific identity.

The subcultures are often regional entities, because the people of a region, as a result of more frequent interactions, tend to think and act alike. But subcultures also take the form of religions, nationalities, fraternal orders, and other institutional complexes which provide a broad identification for people who may otherwise be strangers. The subcultures of a person play a large role in his attitude formulation and become another important predictor of certain values he is likely to hold.

Social Class

People become differentiated not only horizontally but also vertically through a division of labour. The society becomes stratified socially on the basis of wealth, skill, and power. Sometimes castes develop in which the members are reared for certain roles, or social classes develop in which the members feel empathy with others sharing similar values and economic circumstances.

Because social class involves different attitudinal configurations, it becomes a useful independent variable for segmenting markets and predicting reactions. Significant differences have been found among different social classes with respect to magazine readership, leisure activities, food imagery, fashion interests, and acceptance of innovations...

Reference Groups

There are groups in which the individual has no membership but with which he identifies and may aspire to – reference groups. Many young boys identify with big-league baseball players or astronauts, and many young girls identity with Hollywood starts. The activities of these popular heroes are carefully watched and frequently imitated. These reference figures become important transmitters of influences, although more along faces of taste and hobby than basic attitudes.

Face-to-face Groups

Groups that have the most immediate influence on a person's tastes and opinions are face-to-face groups. This includes all the small "societies" with which he comes into frequent contact: his family, close friends, neighbours, fellow workers, fraternal associates, and so forth. His informal group memberships are influenced largely by his occupation, residence, and stage in the life cycle.

The powerful influence of small groups on individual attitudes has been demonstrated in a number of social psychological experiments. Thee is also evidençe that this influence may be growing. David Riesman and his coauthors have pointed to signs which indicate a growing amount of other-direction, that is, a tendency for individuals to be increasingly influenced by their peers in the definition of their values rather than by their parents and elders.

For the marketer, this means that brand choice may increasingly be influenced by one's peers. For such products as cigarettes and automobiles, the influence of peers is unmistakable.

The role of face-to-face groups has been recognized in recent industry campaigns attempting to change basic product attitudes. For years the milk industry has been trying to overcome the image of milk a s "satisfied" drink by portraying its use in social and active situations. The men's wear industry is trying increase male interest in clothes by advertisements indicating that business associates judge a man by how we he dresses.

Of all face-to-face groups, the person's family undoubtedly plays the largest and most enduring role in basic attitude formation. From them he acquires a mental set not only toward religion and politics, but also toward thrift, chastity, food, human relations, and so forth, Although he often rebels against parental values in his teens, he often accepts these values eventually Their formative influences on his eventual attitudes undeniably great.

Family members differ in the types of product messages they carry other family members. Most of what parents know about cereals, candy and toys comes from their children. The wife stimulates family consideration of household appliances, furniture, and vacations. The husband tends to stimulate the fewest purchase ideas, with the exception of the automobile and perhaps the home.

The marketer must be alert to what attitudinal configurations dominant indifferent types of families, and also to how these change over time, For example, the parent's conception of the child's rights and privileges undergone a radical shift in the last 30 years. The child has become the center of attention and orientation in a great number of households leading some writers to label the modern family a "filiarchy." This is important implications not only for how to market to today's family, be also on how to market to tomorrow's family when the indulged child today becomes the parent.

The Person

Social influences determine much but not all of the behavioural variations in people Two individuals subject to the same influences are not likely to have identical attitudes, although these attitudes will probably converge at more points than those of two strangers selected at random. Attitudes are really the product of social forces interacting with the individual's unique temperament and abilities.

Furthermore, attitudes do not automatically guarantee certain types of behaviour. Attitudes are predispositions felt by buyers before they enter the buying process the buying process itself is a learning experience and can lead to a change in attitudes.

Alfred Politz noted t one time that women stated a clear preference for G.E refrigerators over Frigidaire, but that Frigidaire continued to outsell G.E. the answer to this paradox was that preference was only one factor entering into behavior. When the consumer preferring G.E. actually undertook to purchase a new refrigerator, her curiosity led her to examine the other brands. Her perception was sensitized to refrigerator advertisements, sales arguments, and different product features. This led to learning and a change in attitudes.

The Hobbesian Organisational-Factors Model

The foregoing models throw light mainly on the behaviour of family buyers.

But what of the large number of people who are organisational buyers? They are engaged in the purchase of goods not for the sake of consumption, but for further production or distribution. Their common denominator is the fact that they (1) are paid to make purchases for others and (2) operate within an organizational environment.

How do organizational buyers make their decisions? There seem to be two competing views. Many marketing writers have emphasized the predominance of rational motives in organizational buying. Organizational buyers are represented as being most impressed by cost, quality, dependability, and service factors. They are portrayed as dedicated servants of the organization, seeking to secure the best terms. This view has led to an emphasis on performance and use characteristics in much industrial advertising.

Other writers have emphasized personal motives in organizational buyer behaviour. The purchasing agent's interest to do the best for his company is tempered by his interest to do the best for himself. He may be tempted to choose among salesmen according to the extent they entertain or offer gifts. He may choose a particular vendor because this will ingratiate him with certain company officers. He may shortcut his study of alternative suppliers to make his work day easier.

In truth, the buyer is guided by both personal and group goals; and this is the essential point. The political model of Thomas Hobbes comes closest of any model to suggesting the relationship between the two goals. Hobbes held that man is "instinctively" oriented toward preserving ad enhancing his own well-being. But this would produce a 'war of every man against everyman." This fear leads men to unite with others in a corporate body. The corporate man tries to steer a careful course between satisfying his own needs and those of the organization.

Marketing Applications of Hobbesian Model

The import of the Hobbesian model is that organizational buyers can be appealed to on both personal and organization grounds. The buyer has his private aims, and yet he tries to do a satisfactory job for his corporation. He will respond to persuasive salesmen and he will respond to rational product arguments. However, the best "mix" of the two is not a fixed quantity; it varies with the nature of the product, the type of organization and the relative strength of the two drives in he particular buyer.

Where there is substantial similarity in what suppliers offer in the way of products, price, and service, the purchasing agent has less basis for rational choice. Since he can satisfy his organizational obligations with anyone of a number of suppliers, he can be swayed by personal motives. On the other hand, where there are pronounced differences among the competing vendors' products, the purchasing agent is held more accountable for his choice and probably pays ore attention to rations factors. Short-run personal gain becomes less motivating than the long-run gain which comes from serving the organisation with distinction.

The marketing strategist must appreciate these goal conflicts of the organizational buyer. Behind all the ferment of purchasing agents develop standards and employ value analysis lies their desire to a being thought of as order-clerks, and to develop better skills in recording personal and organizational objectives.

Summary

Think back over the five different behavioural models of how the buy translates buying influences into purchasing responses.

Marshallian man is concerned chiefly with economic cues—pries and income—and makes a fresh utility calculation before each purchase.

Pavlovian man behaves in a largely habitual rather than thoughtful way; certain configurations of cues will set off the same behaviour because of rewarded learning in the past.

Freudian man's choices are influenced strongly by motives and fantasies which take place deep within his private world.

Verblenian man acts in a way which is shaped largely by past and present social groups.

And finally, Hobbesian man seeks to reconcile individual

gain with organizational gain.

Thus, it turns out that the "black box" of the buyer is not so black after all. Light is thrown in various corners by these models. Yet no one has succeeded in putting all these pieces of truth together into one coherent instrument for behavioural analysis. This, of course, is the goal of behavioural science.

14

THE IMPORTANCE OF CONVENIENCE IN CONSUMER PURCHASING

Both product and convenience costs influence consumer purchasing behaviour. The increased importance consumers are attaching to convenience offers a key to understanding consumer shopping behaviour and is a major opportunity for markets. Consumer valuation of several forms of convenience is discussed, with special attention devoted to place convenience.

Two factor are of utmost importance in understanding consumer shopping behaviour. First, consumers making shopping decisions achieve an equilibrium between commodity costs and convenience costs. Second, convenience costs are assuming more importance as patronage determinants.

Commodity costs are defined as the monetary price paid the seller to obtain possession of goods and services. Convenience costs are incurred through the expenditure of time, physical and nervous energy, and money required to overcome the frictions of space and time, and to obtain succession of goods and services. For instance, a consumer shopping in the business district spends time, energy, and frequently carfare or working fees, in addition to commodity expenditures. Such costs have always been involved in trading decisions. The new emphasis on conscience does not necessarily mean that consumers are less price conscious formerly, rather, insistence on convenience cost minimization has been superimposed on the desire for economically favourable commodity transactions.

Shopping Costs

The question of consumer time expenditures for shopping is an interesting one. t has been estimated that there is a minimum of five billion adult leisure hours each week in the United States. This reflects is part a population consensus to accept a substantial share of the benefits of the production and marketing revolutions in increased leisure. Paradoxically, the increase in leisure time has been accompanied by a reaction against spending much of that leisure shopping. The modern family is confronted with too many more attractive possible uses of time.

Many forces favour higher consumer valuations of leisure and other convenience considerations. The suburban population movement with is living habit changes and broader family interests is one such force s urban areas also, fundamental social forces are operating which has resulted in families functioning more as a group than as individuals is certain activities, even to the extent of buying together. Such force favouring higher convenience cost valuations include the large numbers of working housewives, the age group imbalance within the population, and higher educational levels. Consumer estimates of purchasing costs are determined by the evaluations of alternative trading and social opportunities. Purchase decisions are made at the point whether total of commodity and convenience costs are considered minimal.

On the supply side sellers are operating in what seems to be a increasingly stanc'ardized production and legal matrix which is tending as limit price competition. The relatively narrow price spread among most retailers carrying identical nationally advertised merchandise suggests new importance for convenience costs in the strategy determination sellers. It appears reasonable to speculate that the range of competition advantage based on commodity costs will narrow. In this setting, it probable that onvenience considerations will assume more importance determinants of purchase behaviour and seller strategy, and that more the competition of the future will focus on convenience considerations will assume more importance determinants of purchase behaviour and seller strategy, and that more the competition of the future will focus on convenience consideration.

Ten Convenience Forms

The importance of convenience as a determinant of consumer acceptance of products and services can be observed in an increasingly range of convenience features built into new products and in new convenience form appearing in the marketing system. Charles G. Mortine President of the General Foods Corporation, has described ten forms convenience which the American consumer now expects almost as a matter of course.

1. Form Convenience – cigarettes in various sizes and tips, and vet-pocket radios.
2. Time Convenience – typified by evening hours, and fresh fruits and vegetables out of season.
3. Place Convenience – file insurance in airline terminals, drive-it-yourself automobile rental services; and the planned shopping center.
4. Quantity or Unit convenience – aspirin in tins of 12, or bottles of 500; an small pianos for the smaller home.
5. Packaging convenience – disposable and utility packages; and the packaged vacation plan. The packaged home is already on the market.
6. Readiness convenience – instant coffee; pre-cooked foods; and The Reader's Digest.
7. Combination Convenience – do it yourself kits; and combination and matched sets.
8. Automatic Operations Convenience – automatic kitchen equipment; power steering and brakes on automobiles; and automation in many fields
9. Selection Convenience – the new variety of dairy products;

and automobile color combinations.

10. Credit Convenience-cars; homes; vacation cruises; and education on credit.

Four Aspects of Place Convenience

Sellers should study all ten convenience forms to find areas in which consumer convenience costs may be reduced. This article is concerned specifically with place convenience. In maximizing place convenience advantages, sellers have related decisions at for levels to make about the capital positions that products ideally should occupy in the market.

(1) The geographic area or areas in which the goods or services are to be offered must be selected. In these areas or markets are found the consumers of the goods. This seller decision usually is not of concerned to the shopper who may choose from the offering of many sellers of substitute products.

The shopping mobility of consumers has tended to be limited to one metropolitan area, but this may not be the case in the future. Perhaps larger scale retailers may become concerned about competition between metropolitan areas as well as with competition within a metropolitan area. For instance, it may represent the same expenditure of convenience costs for a West Hartford resident to order by mail from Hartford, r even to make the trip to downtown Hartford. Conceivably, Hartford department store could become concerned about the drawing power of New York, Boston, and Providence department stores, as well as competition form suburban Hartford stores.

On the other hand, as metropolitan areas grow together to form urban regions, the primate cities of New York, Chicago, and Los Angeles are likely to lose some of their retail leadership to burgeoning regional and provincial metropolitan areas. This may occur in the same fashion, and for much the same reasons, that the central business district has lost ground to suburban elements in the retail structure.

(2) The most satisfactory positions within the market must be selected from those offered by distributors and retailers selling

space in the market Channel-of-distribution decisions are involved. The one-stop shopping tendency of consumers has made channel selection more difficult for sellers in today's fluid market.

(3) Choices must be made among competing retail and wholesale institutions offering access to the customer. Should a full service hole sale be utilized, or would a limited function wholesaler represent a better channel choice? Are urban or suburban positions preferred? What is the role of the shopping centre?

The planned shopping centre movement can be rationalized with some justification in terms of consumer convenience. At the same time, planned centers are more than devices for convenient shopping or mechanisms for retail sales expansion in suburban areas. Planned shopping centers are a basic part of the restructuring of metropolitan communities. Their long-term importance to the economy is based on a continuing reassessment in consumers of shopping and social activities. Consumer convenience is still probably the basis of the shopping center movement. But the social economic, and architectural concepts underlying planned centers as geared to a new kind of social pattern and to what maybe an eruption into a new American social dimension in which consumer desires still require new patterns of marketing.

(4) Problems of positioning of goods within outlets must be settled Display and layout decisions are involved at this level. An experiment by Alfred Politiz Suggests the importance of convenience within the store studying the anatomy of the sale, he purchased and operated a large hardware store in Tampa, Florida. He found that if a product is sufficient well known to get consumer acceptance and is conveniently location the consumer will buy it in preference to a better known product. Why the customer will not select a product he has not heard about, "the little bit of inconvenience wipes out the impressiveness of even the known brands."

Conflicting Cost Considerations

A dominant characteristic of consumer goods marketing at

present the state of flux of consumer valuations of commodity and conveniences costs. While such developments as the discount house reflect strong consumer interest in the reduction of commodity costs, it is quite possible that convenience costs will increase in importance as patronage determinants for more low dollar value items. This will pose anew one of the most challenging problems facing retailers in our complex distribution system: offering the right mix of convenience and economy to customers. Rich rewards may go to merchants able to do this successfully. A wedding of the shopping center concept and the discount house idea represents one promising approach.

Convenience cost pressures are likely to affect more marketing agencies in the future. Some of the possible impacts on planned shopping centers an established business districts are suggested below.

Convenience forces and the Retail structure

Planned Center Increase

The shopping center movement is so new that currently two-thirds of existing centers are less than five years old. This fact, together with the predicted center expansion, indicated that the full impact of the movement has yet to be felt. A fundamental change in the retail structure of metropolitan communities seems certain, as a result of shopping center growth. Over 10,000 planned shopping centers are now in operation. Estimates have been made that by 1975, 17,500 of them will be operating. This means a planned shopping center for each 14,000 of a projected 1975 population of 245 million. This expansion is not expected to be uninterrupted. Many poorly planned intermediate centers are particularly velnerable to new competition.

Individual stores and shopping centers are tending to be larger. Department store branches of 300,000 square feet, and super markets of 50,000square feet have already appeared. A minimum site for regional centers seed to be considered fifty acres. Regional center developers are now thinking in terms of one hundred acres as a minimum site. Tracts of this extremely expensive, especially if they are in or near large cities. The increasing size of regional centers may mean that in the future such centers will be located farther from large population concentrations, and center the suburban periphery.

Consumer convenience considerations also set a limit to the growth of individual stores and centers. For instance, it is generally agreed that shoppers resist walking more than 600 feet from their parked cars to the latest center store. With planned centers, this suggests a limit for the maximum-parking distance that can be used before the planned center its advantages over unplanned shopping districts.

The Distance Concept and Convenience

The distance concept involves time-cost elements rather than a purely special one. High speed roads enabling consumers to travel farther from home on shopping trips are changing consumer views on distance. IN our society of automobile-borne suburbanites, distance between metropolitans point swill increasingly be judged on a time basis, not a mileage basis. The impact of this on established retail patterns is already evident. Downtown retailers have had to compete aggressively for suburban business is order to hold a satisfactory market position. Effective downtown competition for suburban trade is still possible. Indeed, a pattern for the rehabilitation of central business districts has developed. It includes improving access traffic, and parking conditions; modernizing physical facilities; conducting imaginative promotions; and strengthening mass transportation. In short, it means restoring some of the lost convenience aspects to center business district shopping.

Changing Functions in the Metropolitan Retail Structure

The central business district and suburban shopping center provide essential but different services to the community. Retail functions within the central business district and the other elements of the metropolitan retail structure are being modified. Store locations are shifting in the inner core, inner belt, and outer belt of the central business district and miss business thoroughfares. Similarly, retailers in planned an unplanned secondary commercial sub-districts, neighborhood business streets, small store clusters, and planned regional shopping centers are modifying functions to adapt to the needs of consumers living and shopping overall wide area. The downtown are may respond by becoming more of a business service, and recreational center and less of a mercantile one opinions as this vary widely. Frank Lloyd Wright visualizes the city of the future without a central shopping district. Others anticipate a downtown stimulated in part by shopping center competition, which will furthermore downtown property owners and merchants into rehabilitation and redesign programmes.

Other Dimensions of Convenience

In addition to spatial and temporal aspects, convenience has social and esthetic dimensions. This is one reason shopping center are likely to play an increasingly important role in community social-life. All shopping centers are likely to benefit by following a policy of community identification although the benefits are particularly apparent with the large community and regional centers. Auditoriums, meeting rooms, restaurants, and other facilities making shopping more convenient are found in more planned centers. As more planned centers include such amenity shopping centers may come to resemble earlier market places, which served social as well as trading functions.

Consumers favour centers in which merchandise is presented conveniently, informally, and interestingly. Shopping-center planning, therefore, the excitement and pleasure to shopping. The modified bazaar concept of the center is likely to gain favour as weather-controlled centers without window displays and partitions come into being. For instance, Southdale, the new regional center outside Minneapolis, has a glass enclosed mall connecting the various stores in the center.

Convenience and New Retail Types

New store types are likely to appear in planned centers. Since shopping centers are located on choice, relatively low cost land compared to downtown stores, one floor retailing operations are possible to an extent not practical downtown. This may mean a reduction in handling costs and in the number of people needed to conduct and supervise operations. Some specialty store in planned centers should be in a position to offer more variety in prices and styles than down town specialty stores operating in less space.

Convenience pressures may provide a stimulus for other retailing developments offering lower convenience costs to consumers. Among these maybe increased direct-to-consumer selling, catalogue and telephone willing, perhaps a combination of television and telephone selling, and automatic vending machines. Improved vending equipment selling an increasing broad variety of merchandise could turn some planned centers and store clusters into round-the-clock merchandising machines.

Metropolitan for Decision Making

Understanding of the current state of the art requires acceptance of change itself as the dominant characteristic of marketing. If understanding of the process of market change, the forces producing change, and therefore, ability to develop policies under accelerated change condition is to be increased, more attention to the convenience aspects of marketing seems justified.

Measurement of convenience costs, while difficult, is not impossible Reillys Law represents one approach to quantifying some convenience dynamics, which beganin1927, that retail business gravitated from smaller cities and towns in accordance with a definite law. Reilly based has law of retail gravitation on two rules. The first is that, the larger the city the more outside trade it will draw. The second rule is that a city draw more trade from nearby towns than distant ones.

Reilly's contribution was in providing a quantitative measure of the rate that trade increases as the population of a city increases. His law of retail gravitation follows: Two cities attract retail trade from any intermediate city or town in the vicinity of the breaking point approximately in direct proportion to the population of the two cities and in inverse proportion to the square of the distances (via most direct in proved automobile highway) from these two cities to the intermediate town.

The law can be supplemented by discounts based on surveys, observations to obtain approximations of convenience cost consideration in trade areas. Factors such as time expenditures, distance (including distance to the store and with the store), and intervening shopping opportunities can be isolated in individual experiments. Development of consumer-distance concept to measure the costs of various locations possible. This could be based on the number of consumers within an multiples by driving time minutes from a location. But the core convenient analysis lies in the area of consumer psychology and sociology. This means that marketers will have to absorb more of what the and other disciplines, in addition to economics, have to contribute marketing theory.

15

MARKET SEGMENTATION AND CONSUMER BEHAVIOUR

In addition to the number of consumers and their incomes, the distribution of consumers over space is important to marketers. Changes in population distribution are producing important economic social, and marketing consequences. Interurbia is defined as "as agglomeration of cities and surrounding, densely populated, non farm counties," Marketers have a vital interests in the commercial impact of interurbia, and in the problems and opportunities created by this new population distribution pattern. Interurbian psychology and advertising media factors are discussed.

Interurbia: The Changing Face of America

Background

As a nation, we did not reckon with the pace of our growth. The quickened pace of our population growth has caused the Census Bureau to increase its forecast for 1965 by four million...its 1976 forecast by over 7 million.

The dimensions of the automobile boom were not foreseen either. In 1953, hard-boiled automotive economists forecast 50 million cars on the road by 1959. The fact is the 58,591,000 cars were registered in 1959. This forecasting error of approximately 8.6 million cars represents about half the passenger cars in Western Europe.

We failed to anticipate many factors that affect housing. By the late nineteen-forties, we did include playgrounds in city apartments built for young families. But we did not foresee the number of cars they would buy. And we did not reckon with the demand for television sets, automatic washing machines, and air conditioners that made these building electrically obsolete while they were still new. Most serious of almost city apartments do not have enough bedrooms for the baby crop. So the young families move out to the suburbs.

But they aren't much better off in the suburbs either. There are enough bedrooms of babies in the typical two-bedroom house built in this '40's. And many lack garages and carports. Young owners invest million trying to expand their little homes. Many give up and move out. Thanks to the automobile and the rise in real income, they can move still further from town, to find more space in the far suburbs in new homes they soon outgrow once again.

Business planers in the suburbs also failed to anticipate our growth. Many post-war shopping centers allowed only two square feet of parking space for every square foot of selling space. But today often ratio of firm square feet to one square foot is required.

As a result..

The 600-mile city arrives unherablded.

One of the main characteristics of this dynamic growth is the rapid evolution of the now-familiar phenomenon known as Suburbia into as infinitely more complex social pattern now known as INTERURBIA.

The most graphic demonstration of this evolution is in New York City. There, as elsewhere, it is no longer quite realistic to speak of a city and is suburbs. The New York metropolitan area has long been a conglomeration of many cities and many suburbs. Interms of population and physics plant, the "city" goes beyond the already obsolete limits of the New York metropolitan area. Indeed, it is no longer a Greater New York of a Greater Boston, Philadelphia, Baltimore or Washington. It is virtually about 600-mile city from Maine to Virginia. Actually, there are only two stretches in this 600-mile city—one of 2 miles, the other of 17 miles which are not part of metropolitan areas. And while this 600-mile "city" comprises less than 2 per cent of its nation's land area, it represents 24 per cent of its retail sales.

Interurbia, by definition, has these characteristics: it contains two more adjacent metropolitan areas with either two cities of 100,000 more, or one city of 100,000 and 3 cities of 25,000 or more, plus adjacent counties with less than 25 per cent farm population and more than 100 people per square mile.

There are now 14 of these Interurbias in the U.S. based on the last Census—plus two Interurbias in the making in the Southwest. They dot the landscape of the Eastern Seaboard, Midwest, Southwest and Pacific Coast. Together they account of or almost half of the country's population of 178 million and for more than half of its retail sales, yet they stand on less than 4 per cent of the country's total land. Within these fourteen interurbias, an average of 620 people live in every square mile—over 12 times as many people per square mile as there are in the rest of the country.

There are also some areas that did not at the last censure quite fit the definition of an Interurbia, but that almost certainly will fit it soon.

One of these is long the Florida coast and across the middle of the peninsula. North of Miami the coastal strips is already filled in for many miles. A big Interurbian growth is now under way south of Tampa and is beginning to touch the Fort Myers area. By 1965, this Interurbia will probably account for two thirds of the population of Florida.

Another potential Interurbia is to be found in the Piedmont area. So far this long chain of cities has reflected only the first stage of urbanization. Cities have grown faster than surrounding country. And there are long groups of open country between many of the cities. But the area is growing letter than the states it lies in and shows signs of becoming an Interurbia in the near future.

What has Caused Our Cities to Merge

The plantation is quite simple, although the results are incredibly complicated. What has happened is that homes and jobs, at one time closely tied to each other and firmly fixed in their places, have both been made movable—as tough at the end of increasingly long ropes.

The central fact which distinguishes Interurbia from suburbia is that that labour force does not move in a steady one-way stream, but more in a prices of cross currents. Westport, Connecticut, in Northeastern Interurbia serves as an example.

Most people commuting from West port move southwesterly to New York, but a significant percentage commute to Bridgeport, and New York. And Westport itself also receives part of its own labour force from Connecticut, nearby New York and the surrounding countryside.

The emergence of Interurbia from the now out-dated concept of city, and country has been stimulated more by the growth of satellite cities than it has from the big central city. The Interurbia in the Chicago and Milwaukee area or strip serves to illustrate this fact.

Between 1930 and 1959 the population in the suburban areas between Chicago and Milwaukee proper has increased 95 per cent while the cities themselves have increased 17 per cent. The same is true of the retail sales. In the areas between Chicago-Milwaukee, retail sales in 1959 were 460 per cent greater than in 1930, while in the two cities themselves, retail sales had increased 167 per cent.

What is true in the suburban areas in the Chicago-Milwaukee strip appears to be true of the entire country. In 1958, dollar sales per capita in the Interurbian suburbs were, on the average, 68 per cent higher than in the other suburbs of the country.

Interurbia in 1975

As we look to the future, we can with some confidence, predict the day is not too far distant when most of our people will be passed within Interurbia – as most of our sales now are. In 1975, it is estimated that Interurbia will represent 60 per cent of our population 70 per cent of retail sales.

Our 600-mile city in the Northeast may well grow toward the paramount. Its arm now creeping up the Hudson, will in all probability with Cleveland, Detroit, and Chicago, and stretch down Illionois to Louis. That would be an Interurbia about twice the length of the Atlantic strip – a city more than 1,200 miles long.

On the West Coast, the future holds the distinct possibility of an urban strip stretching northward from San Diego and connecting somewhere in the Caligornia Valley with the southward movement from San Francisco and the Bay area.

In the South, Dallas and Fort Worth extend in one direction down to Housston and Galveston, and in another, through Waco and Austin to San Antonio.

People will, as in the past, settle close to water ways, whether they be ocean, lake, river, or canal; but there will be other motivations, too – climate, the need for land and, as always, the desire for better living.

How Interurbia may affect Our Way of Living

Beneath the shell of uniform mass housing there most likely will be a series of different communities each catering to a different age and income group. The trend toward physical uniformity is rating a counter desire to be socially different. And this desire to be different is already apparent in some of the ostensibly homogeneous suburbs a such as the Levittowans in the East and in Park Forest, south of Chicago.

Families are on the move. More and more people are leaving the old home town – in a series of moves – from home won to college, from college to a great organization, and then from one provincial outpost to another, until finally comes the day whe the man is summoned home to Rome.

The old home town may look pretty much the same. Yet if you check the leadership in the traditional town, you will find that the sons of the "early" families have more often than not left to join the transient life. Someone else, very much like them, is now sitting in the place they might have had in the Junior Chamber of commerce, the Community Chest, or the Greens Committee of the Country Club.

Then there is the more familiar kind of mobility—the great exodus from the city to the country. Familiar, yes, except that the exodus does not necessarily consist of just one jump—from city to suburbs.

To illustrate: since the war, there has been a tremendous growth in row-house developments in Northeast Philiadelphia. Socially, however, for many of these people there is still another transition to be made. For all their boasting about what a wonderful place the "5600" block is, the unspoken goal is to move out of the city. If the husband gets that raise, the "For Sale' sign goes up.

Mobility breeds more mobility. Once a person has learned to change environment it becomes easier to adapt to another. The good transient is professional about this.

Another aspect of this mobility is the tremendous upgrading urge it produces. One of the most characteristic complaints to be found in the new villages of Interurbia is about the quality of goods they have in the stores. The complaint usually takes the lines of 'who-do-they-thing-we-are-anyway?"

The most interesting thing about this upgrading urge is how very much it is conditioned by the immediate group in which a couple find themselves.

It is the group in Interurbia that determines when a luxury becomes a necessity. Take something like an automatic dryer. When only a few housewives in a block have one, other housewives can take it or leave it. As more and more housewives follow suit, it soon becomes an almost unsocial act not to own one.

Finally only the most resolute can hold out. This use to improve one's own status has caused the developer of one of the new suburbs to suggest somewhat facetiously building a "life cycle suburb." You would live in one court as a child, a two bedroom apartment as a newlywed: then a ranch house; final, then you're old and gray, and your children are scattered to the four winds, you would move back to a court to serve out your term as a baby sitter.

Interurbian Psychology

Do the psychological needs of the people living in Interurbia difficult from those in the rest of the country? They do most decidedly. Here from a special study of several thousand people, are the principal derives of these Interurbian people and some idea a to how they may differ five the rest of the population.

The Interurbian man is significantly above the national average in his expressed desire for achievement—his desire to rival and surpass others—to do hi best—to achieve prestige and acclaim. He has an equally pronounced need to dominate other people. He wants to be a leader influence others. The Interurbian man is more willing to talk about and less strict in his attitudes.

Our Interurbian man likes also to be the center of attention—to have others notice him-to make an impression on others. In short, vanity and self-dramatization are stronger needs in him than they are in the living elsewhere in our land. Change he doesn't mind. In fact, tour Interest bian man likes to do new and different things...to change his daily routine. He likes variety and novelty. Possibly this is a key as to why accepts the need for mobility with such calm.

It is a fact of great significance in the development of future advertising appeals that the characteristics which are most highly developed in the men and women of Interurbia are those on which so many great advertising success stories have been built and will be built. The people of Interurbia might be said to represent a pre-conditioned audience for the skillful advertising of many products and services to a greater degree than the people outside Interurbia.

How Interurbia Stimulates and Stabilizes our Economy Interurbia will push us toward a national economy that certainly will be bigger, and probably more stable. The stability will be due to the changing pattern of ownership and consumption interurbia imposes. Except for a little furniture and a closet full of clothes, most Interurbia city dwellers have no passions. New York city, for example, accounts for only three per cent of the nation's automobiles, but represents 15 per cent of the country's restaurant sales.

By contrast, the Interurbiate who has left the big city is forced to become a man of property. His ownership of a house creates a hunger for hard goods that inevitably drives him into hard work more relentlessly than the metropolitan dweller.

For example, one large builder found that the purchase of every new home automatically created 17 other purchases, such as furniture, appliances, curtains, garden tools, a new car-even a second car.

The stabilizing influence of Interurbia also arises from the huge spending programme on the part of businesses, utilities and public authorities that interurbia demands. And Interurbia's need for new highways alone is accelerating the need for housing in a brutally direct fashion. The present highway construction programme calls for the destruction or removal of about 90,000 houses a year—just to build roads!

Still another stabilizing influence lies in the increased opportunity for workers to maintain employment by being more mobile.

While the automobile has become the symbol of many Inerurbian problems, it fills a basic need. The phenomenon of Interurbia is based on the mobility supplied by the private car to drive miles to shopping center school, church and job. If anything, the need for this mobility will grow as business and homes spread further out.

But the growing use of the automobile is outstripping the ability of the central city to cope with it. In fact, the congestion has become so overpowering that some planners are persuaded that the means taken to open the choked downtown arteries are mere expedients. Some are bold enough to predict a not-too-distant day when the private car is barred altogether from the metropolitan city, as an improved intra-city barred altogether from the metropolitan city, as an improved intra-city transit system takes on the job of moving people about faster than they are now moving.

New Marketing Problems

The marketing problems created by Interurbia will be no less complex. With 31,000,000 changes of residence every year, the retailer worrying about new locations will have to keep a close watch on consumer movements.

The friendly neighbourhood dealer may lose some of his old sales punch as he sees new faces among his customers more often than before.

The manufacturer may find that the Central Cities in Interurbia are no longer the focus of marketing, but somewhere in between. Test marketing may be expanded to Interurbian strips, instead of individual markets. The same may be true do product research.

Sales organizations may grow smaller, as they concentrate more retail service. The two-thousand-man sales force may become a thing of the past.

Executives in charge of areas with traditional designations such as New England, Middle Atlantic, may be re-assigned to supervise a particular Interurbian strip.

New stores, service stations, and discount houses will expose customers to brands they've never seen before. As New York and Boston toward each other in the nation's largest Interurbia, they carry with these certain brands that New London, Connecticut, had never herd of. That same may apply to prices. Discount houses will introduce some cut price hitherto unknown to various communities along the way.

The Interurbian shopper for a refrigerator or other hard goods may soon be shopping in a retail store which carries no stock except the needed for demonstration or display. The retailer will simply phone in order to a warehouse, and the model ordered will be on the truck delivered to the customer's house within a matter of hours.

This new convenience for the retail shopper within Interurbia will made possible through a mammoth warehouse system handling may brands and a variety of product. It is conceivable, for example, that the hard-goods' needs of Northeast Interurbia alone could be efficiently supplied by four or five such warehouses.

The Interurbian influence can already be detected in the marketing procedures of many important good chains. The central city is no longer the sole location for their warehousing and buying. Rather their never centers have either moved out from eh metropolitan area, or they are being duplicated out in the growing Interurbian territory.

Even today, in major chains like Kroger and Colonial stores, we find some warehouse buying headquarters outside the central city with well developed "spokes" that are completely independent of any historic city or political boundaries.

As we change from the old concept of a metropolitan marketing area to a new Intrurbian marketing area, perhaps we should re-examine the traditional methods by which we separate and study our markets.

Perhaps it may not be too early for market research firms to break down their findings on the basis of interurbia versus non-Interurbia.

Advertising Media in Interurbia

Concentration of population has virtually always meant lower advertising costs. The bigger the mass of circulation an advertiser buyers, the lower the relative cost to him.

Today the space an advertiser buys in a country weekly can cost him ten times as much per unit of circulation as the space in a large daily. As interurbia develops, this discrepancy may be narrowed – with increased efficiency in advertising expenditure.

In the new Interurbia, the metropolitan daily may, of necessity, become less and less identified with the central city of Interurbia, and more with Interurbia as a whole. One ay of accomplishing this is to publish more zoned editions, as some large dailies are already doing.

The smaller dailies and weeklies may stand to benefit from the Interurbian development in two ways: first, they are in the happy position of serving their readers come to them; secondly, the pattern of marketing is changing so fast that major chain stores are becoming less and less identified with the central city, as they develop new spokes in their marketing wheel.

Interurbia also presents a challenge to Sunday supplements, whose substantial post-war growth has been based on their ability to provide coverage of the large metropolitan centers. More and more, the supplements may find it beneficial to buttress their circulation in the medium-size cities between their present major metropolitan markets. This would enable them to provide the same intensive coverage of the Interurbian areas that they now provide in central cities.

Today some 70 national magazines representing 71% of all audited magazine circulation accept advertising for circulation covering individual regions or markets. This trend of magazines toward regional adverting may gain further momentum as more advertisers begin to look at circulations for whole Interurbias, and not just their metropolitan segments. In so doing, they will find in many cases that the traditionally broad-base magazines can cover as many or more families within Interurbia as some of the individual local media that they have used traditionally.

TV set ownership throughout Interurbia will increase to something close to the 90 per cent that now exists in metropolitan areas. But TV network structures still lag behind the Interurbian development due to their historical tie to individual markets. Thus an advertiser seeking coverage of Northeastern Interurbia would have to supplement his ten network stations with several spot stations. Further network requirements for "must-buy" TV stations may be related more directly to Interurbias.

Radio's future welfare in Interurbia may rest in part on it

becoming more and more a vehicle for news and music—an economical type of programming which could help keep costs competitive with TV. The degree to which smaller local stations within Interurbia are used will depend, as in the case of small dailies and weeklies, on the saturation required in the new areas which retailers are cultivating.

In closing...

We are at the foothills of a way of life which will require a more intensive study than we have ever given it before...a study of people's motivations and desires... of how they live and why they live as they do. And we must learn all this before it is too late.

Of one thing we are certain as we center this new way of life; that Interurbia will produce fundamental changes. And as it does, probably to one of us will be able to do business as we have been doing it. No one will find paradise in Interurbia. Paradise will always be just around the comes. And that for all of us may be our greatest opportunity.

16

CONSUMER MARKETS: FAMILIES BY AGE

Current demographic and economic information is essential to effective marketing management. Changes in demography not only affect the structure of market demand, but also have far-reaching implications for such marketing decisions as product design and media selection. A review of important socioeconomic characteristics at various stages of the family life cycle is presented.

Families by Age I: Characteristics

A striking 90 per cent of the growth in the nation's family population expected during the Sixties will be accounted for by the relatively young and the relatively old—by families under 30 and those over 55. In the preceding 10-year span these age groups represented only tow fifths of the total growth.

As these simple statistics suggest, the age composition of our population is being significantly altered. Two major demographic tremors have been working their way through the nations population structure over the past to years. The first shock wave was triggered by the sharp drop in births during the Depression Thirties, the second by the postwar birth boom.

The changing age structure of our population is, of course, of special interest to marketers. Clearly, it is not only affecting the structure of demand, but it also has far-reaching implications for such merchandising decisions as product design and media selection. This article, the first of two, reviews the most current available demographic and economic information on families by age of head. A second story will be concerned with the purchasing patterns of families at various stages of the life cycle.

Family Head Under 25

Households under 25 account for about 5 per cent of the nation's families, not only 3 per cent of all consumer demand. Last year the median earnings of these families came to roughly $4,300, or about 25 per cent below the all-country figure. Three out of every five young couples earned less than $5,000 and barely 15 per cent had over $7,000.

The birth rate at this stage of the family's life cycle is at a peak level. Thus, although they constitute only 5 per cent of the family population these households had 26 per cent of all children born last year. Two thirds of all under-25-year-old homes include children and about 30 per cent have more than one. Nevertheless, well over half of all wives work all or part of the year. A third of all young families live in the central cities of metropolitan areas, and about 20 per cent own their own homes.

Three out of every five family heads of his age have earned high school diplomas, a level of education well above the all-country average. However, fewer youngsters in this age bracket have finished college than in next-oldest grouping. Youngsters who remaining school longer generally marry later.

Family Head 25-34

A fifth of all households and about the same share of the country's spending power are to be found in this age bracket. The median annual income is about normal, and at this age a full third of all families ears more than $7,000. But indebtedness as well as income has increased: two thirds of these families owe money.

Although the birth rate has slowed appreciably at this age

level, to about one new arrival in every four homes annually, over half of all children born last year were to parents in this bracket. Close to 90 per cent of these households include children, and two thirds of them more than one.

As would be expected under these circumstances, relatively fewer wives now work; of those that do, about three in five work the year round. The proportion of families living in the suburbs is far greater than that for the under-25 group. The frequency of home ownership has increased substantially, although it is still under the all-family rate.

This age group is better educated than any other. Close to 15 per cent of the household heads have completed college, and an additional 43 per cent have high school diplomas. Roughly one quarter of all males are employed in professional-technical occupations or are managers and officials. Craftsmen as count for an additional fifth, operatives for another quarter.

Family Head 35-44

The largest proportion of total family spending power—an estimated 27 per cent -is in the hands of this age group, which accounts for a quarter of households. The median family earns well above he norm: close to hall of these homes are in the over $7,000 bracket. The frequency of indebtedness continues in the neighbourhood of two thirds, but the six of outstanding obligations appears to have declined in this bracket.

A very large proportion of these families have children living at home, but fewer households include youngsters under six. Nevertheless, over two fifths of our entire child population is accounted for the 35-44 age bracket.

The ratio of working wives in this group is near the average. The family now appears to be fully rooted, and barely 15 per cent change their residence in the course of a year. The rate of home ownership has increased sharply: two thirds of these families own their homes.

The level of educational achievement is well above average, with one out of every two household heads having completed high school. This is a slightly smaller fraction than in the 25-34 age bracket, as each upcoming generation in recent years has been staying somewhat longer in school than the one preceding.

Family Head 45-54

This the most affluent of all the age groups. Earning capacity at this stage of the life cycle is at its peak. Last year the median income of these families exceeded $7,000. More than a quarter of all homes in this age category have incomes in excess of $10,000. All in all, this group accounts for a fifth of all families but a quarter of all spending power. Only one out of every two of these households in debt.

The proportion of families with children has dipped below 60 per cent. Actually, many of the offspring of these families have by now reached 18 and hence are no longer classified as children in government statistics.

As would be expected, there is a sharp increase at this age level in the proportion of wives who work, and an even greater rise in the number working all year.

The educational level of this age category is substantially below that of the preceding. Most of the family heads in this group were of school age during the depression years of the Thirties. All in all, fewer than two fifths of them achieved a high school diploma.

The occupational mix of this category more or less parallels the factional pattern, except that there are slightly fewer professional and technical persons and some what more managers and officials.

Family Head 55-64

The income pattern in this age bracket reflects the presence of some retired and semi-retired families. There is clustering at both ends of the income scale. Nearly 40 per cent of these families – a substantially larger proportion than found in the 45-54 group – earn below $5,000. At the end of the scale, one fifth of all households, a better than average, have annual incomes exceeding

$10,000. On balance, median are still above par. Indebtedness has dropped sharply, to only about one third of these families.

Only one out of every five of these households includes children. Family size has now declined to 3.0, as compared to an all-family average of 3.7. Also, there are relatively fewer working wives in this group than among younger families. And there apparently has been some moving back into town from the suburbs.

Only slightly better than a quarter of these family heads have completed high school, vehicle a third failed to go the full course in elementary school. Some decline in the ownership of durable goods is in evidence at this stage of the life cycle, sharpest of all in cars. However, three founds of these families still operate automobiles, and one in five has two or more vehicles.

Family Head 65 and above

This is the age of the retired. Median income for this group last year was $3,200, or only slightly better than half the all-family figure. Above 70 per cent of these household shave less than $5,000 a year to spend, wile only about one in ten have over $10,000. In the neighbourhood of 10 per cent of total demand originates with this age bracket, which includes about 15 per cent of all our citizens.

Few of these families still have youngsters living at home. As a matte of fact, there has been a rather substantial change in family composition—fewer husband and wife units, more cases of a man or a woman living with a relative. Close to one fifth of all wives, however, are still working.

A relatively large proportion of families reside outside the urbanize areas, which probably explains the continued high level of home ownership.

The general educational achievement of this group is lower than that of any other: only one out of every five family heads has completed high school. More than two out of every five have failed to complete elementary school. This generation was born in an era in which less emphasis was put on formal training.

A relatively high proportion of this group (20% as compared to national average of only 8%) work on farms. This may reflect the five that while persons employed in industry tend to retire upon coming age, farmers are more likely to continue working on a reduced schedule age, farmers are more likely to continue working on a reduced scheduled. A

Also, in the recent migration away from the land, younger families left relatively large numbers.

There is a further contraction in the proportion of families owner durable goods in this age bracket. Cars are now maintained by less the half of all households.

Families by Age II: Expenditures

The changing age structure of our growing population influence many marketing decisions. Marketing strategies for consumer markets must recognize that shifts in preferences for various goods and services occur as families read successive stages of the life cycle. Families are categories by the age of the family head, and their spending patterns are reported.

Never before in the nation's history—not even during the great immigration early in the century—has the age structure of our adult population gone through as sharp a change as in the present period. We are now experiencing the combined consequences of the sharp fall in births during the depression Thirties and the spectacular baby boom of the prospectors Fifties. All this means a shift in the goods and services that are in demand and has a far-reaching effect on many aspects of merchandising strategy from packaging to the phrasing of the promotion message.

This, the second of two articles on the characteristics of households in each stage in the life cycle, is concerned with spending patterns. The preceding story reviewed social and income traits. The observations the follow are based on the Bureau of Labour Statistics' recent study is spending habits of urban families and single consumers. The complex study covers the years 1960 and 1961; however, the only data related thus far are for the earlier year. This information was collected in metropolitan areas and in 16 small cities. Since a similar survey was conducted in 1950, it is possible to examine the changes in consumer preferences over the past decade. In comparing past and present expenditure patterns, 1950 data have been converted to 1960 dollars.

Head Under 25

The typical consumer unit in this age bracket spent $4,500 for good and services in 1960, or substantially less than the national average aggregate this group accounts for less than 5 per cent of all buying.

A large proportion of people in this bracket are single consumers, a fact reflected in the group's general expenditure profile. The percentage of income that goes for food, clothing, medical and personal care is below the all-country norm. Shelter is a significant item percentage-wise at this age level, although actual dollar outlays for this purpose are below par. Expenditure for automobiles, on the other had, are quite large, both in absolute and relative terms.

A much smaller proportion of the young household'

S budget now goes for food and clothing than did so 10 years ago. Hose furnishings and equipment, too, now make a smaller claim. Spending for housing on the other hand—shelter and particularly home operations—has grown more important than it was in 1950.

Head 25-34

Most of the spending units in this group are husband-wife families. Spending for consumption came to $5,600 in the survey year, which is fractionally above average. This group accounts for close to a fifth of total consumer buying.

Expenditures in this age bracket broadly follow the all-country pattern. The proportion of resources channeled into the home-shelter, household operations and home furnishings—is above par, while outlays food and clothing are slightly below the national average, measured in relative terms, and about equal to the all-household figure in actual dollars. The automobile also takes a somewhat smaller share of total spending, although dollar outlays are higher than they are in the average American family.

The average household in this bracket spends about a quarter more on foods and services than does the typical under-25-year-old family. However, food, alcohol, tobacco and clothing expenditures are much more than 25 per cent greater. (Te consumer unit is bigger now—there are more reasons to feed and clothe.) The rise in outlays for house furnishings, and particularly for autos, is less than for all spending.

As in the case of the youngest families, a substantially smaller share of is gage group's spending now goes for food, clothing and home furnishings than did so a decade ago, while a much greater proportion is for shelter and household operations. Personal and medical care, have increased in importance in this bracket, and more is being spent automobiles.

Head 35-44

Roughly a quarter of total consumer buying is represented by this age group. In the survey year the average household spent about $6,500, more than in any other bracket.

Although more money is now being spent on cars, home furnishing and household operations than in the preceding age group, the increases for these items are less than the increment in all spending. The big rise in outlays is for food and clothing, which account for an above average portion of this age group's budget. This is because, at this stage of the this cycle, and household has reached its peak size.

As observed in connection with the other age groups, food, clothing and home furnishings are less significant percentage wise than age, but shelter, particularly household operations, and the automobile at more important.

Head 45-54

Through the family is now at its peak earning level, expenditures for current consumption have declined moderately, to $6,200. Only above 90 per cent of income after taxes finds its way to the market, as compared 95 per cent for the preceding age category. In large measure this development explained by a decline in household size. Many of the offspring of the families have reached adulthood and left home. However, this age category is of most importance to markets since it accounts for over quarter of all consumer spending.

The decrease in family size is reflected in expenditure habits. Total outlays are roughly 5 per cent below the next-youngest bracket but spending for food, shelter, and the home generally has declined by an even larger proportion. The decrease is also relatively big for automobiles. On the other hand, spending for some items is off by less than 5 per cent. These include medical and personal care. Expenditure for alcohol increases.

Changes in this age group's spending habits over the past decade are special. Food now claims a smaller share of the family's budget, housing personal car a somewhat larger share. The importance of clothing is changed.

Head 55-64

In this age bracket we find some significant changes in the composition of the family, its earnings and its spending habits. While the majority of household heads are at their peak earning capacity, many others and retired or semi-retired. The average family now spends $5,000 for goods and services, or about 85 per cent of post-tax income.

Total consumption of this group is a full fifth less than in the 45-to 54 bracket. Many items, however, are off by much more, notably house furnishings, clothing, recreation, alcohol and automobiles. On the other hand expenditures decline only moderately for medical care, shelter, and household operations. The decrease in food spending is also surprisingly small.

The share of the budget going for food has dropped from 29 per cent to 25 percent in the last 10 years, while the portion devoted to housing has increased largely because of the shelter and operation components. Autos and personal and medical care have become more important since 1950, but the weight assigned to clothing has remained the same.

65 and above

The average household in this retired age bracket spend slightly the $3,200 in the survey year for all goods and services, representing above 90 percent of its post-tax income. About 19 per cent of all consumer units are in the bracket, but they account for only a little better than 11 per cent of total spending. The average household has declined to 1.8 persons.

With the sharp reduction in spending, essentials such as food and housing take a comparatively large share of the budget. Three fifths total outlays go for these items. An additional 12 per cent are for personal and medical care.

Consumption is more than a third less than in the 55-to-64 group. More items, of course, have fallen by much more, notably tobacco and alcohols clothing, house furnishings, transportation and recreation. Among item that have decreased by less than the drop in total spending are house food and medical care.

A decade ago, older families spent a larger share of their budget is food and clothing, but a smaller proportion for housing, than they today. Outlays for medical and personal care are appreciably highly having increased form roughly a tenth of the budget to about an eight.

17

NEW CRITERIA FOR MARKET SEGMENTATION

Segmentation analysis — the evaluation of all potentially useful ways of segmenting a market — may produce a more effective marketing strategy than does segmentation based solely on demographic characteristics. The strategic choice concept of segmentation broadens the scope of marketing planning to include the positioning of new as well as established products. Marketing must develop its own interpretive theory if it is to optimize the value of segmentation analysis.

The director of marketing in a large company is confronted by some of the most difficult problems in the history of U.S. industry. To assist him, the information revolution of the past decade puts at his disposal a vat array of techniques, facts and figures. But without a way to master this information, he can easily be overwhelmed by the reports that flow in to him incessantly from marketing research, economic forecasts, cost analyses, and sales breakdowns. He must have more than mere access to mountains of data. He must himself bring to bear a method of analysis that cuts through the detail to focus sharply on new opportunities.

In this article, I shall propose such as method. It is called segmentation analysis. It is base don the proposition that once you discover the most careful ways of segmenting a market, you have produced the beginnings of a sound marketing strategy.

Unique Advantages

Segmentation analysis has developed out of several key premises:

In today's economy, each brand appears to self effectively to only certain segments of any market and not to the whole market.

Sound marketing objectives depend on knowledge of how segments which produce the most customers for a company's brands differ in requirements and susceptibilities from the segments which produce the largest number of customers for competitive brands.

Traditional demographic methods of market segmentation do not usually provide this knowledge. Analyses of market segments by age, sex, geography, and income level are not likely to provide s much direction for marketing strategy as management requires.

Once the marketing director does discover the most pragmatically useful way of segmenting his market, it becomes a new standard for almost all his evaluations. He will use it to appraise competitive strengths and vulnerabilities, to plan his product line, to determine his advertising and selling strategy, and to set precise marketing objectives against which performance can later be measured, Specifically, segmentation analysis help him to–

...direct the appropriate amounts of promotional attention and money in the most potentially profitable segments of his market;

...design a product line that truly parallels the demands of the market instead of one that bulks in some areas and ignores or scants other potentially quit profitable segments;

...catch the first sign of a major trend in a swiftly changing market and thus give him time to prepare to take advantage of it;

...determine the appeals that will be most effective in his company's advertising; and, where several different appeals are significantly effective quantify the segments of he market responsive to each;

... choose advertising media more wisely and determine the proportion of budget that should be allocated to each medium in he light of anticipated impact;

... correct the timing of advertising and promotional efforts so that they are massed in the weeks, months, and seasons when selling resistance is leant and responsiveness is likely to be at its maximum;

...understand otherwise seemingly meaningless demographic market in formation and apply it in scores of new and effective ways.

These advantages hold in the case of both packaged goods and have goods, and for commercial and industrial products as well as consumer products.

Guide to Strategy

Segmentation analysis cuts through the data facing a marketing director when he tried to set targets based on markets as a whole, or when relies primarily on demographic breakdowns. It is a systematic approved that permits the marketing planner to pick the strategically most important segmentations and then to design brands, products, packages, communications, and marketing strategies around them. It infinitely simplifies the setting of objectives.

In the following sections we shall consider non demographic ways of segmenting markets. These ways dramatize the point that finding marketing opportunities by depending solely on demographic breakdowns is like trying to win a national election by relying only on the information in a census. A modern census contains useful data, but it identifies neither the crucial issues of an election, or those groups whose voting habits are still fluid, nor he needs, values, and attitudes that influence how those groups will vote. This kind of information, rather tan census-type data, is the kind that wins elections – and markets.

Consider, for example, companies like Procter & Gamble, General Motors, or American Tobacco, whose multiple brands sell against one another and must, every day, win new elections in the marketplace:

These companies sell to the whole market, not by offering one brand that appeals to all people, but by covering the different segments with multiple brands. How can they prevent these brands from cannibalizing each other? How can they avoid surrendering opportunities to competitors by failing to provide brands that appeal to all important segments? In neither automobiles, groups, nor cigarettes do demographic analyses reveal to the manufacturer what products to make or what products to sell to what segments of the market. Obviously, some modes of segmentation other than demographic are needed to explain why brands which differ so little nevertheless find their own niches in the market, each one appealing to a different segment.

The on that issue is not that demographic segmentation should be regarded, but rather that it should be regarded as only one among away possible ways of analyzing markets. In fact, the key requirement of segmentation analysis is that the marketing director should never assume is advance that anyone method of segmentation is the bet. His first job should be to must all probable segmentation and then choose the most meaningful ones to work with. This approach is analogous to that used in search in the physical sciences, where the hypothesis that best seems to explain the phenomena under investigation is the one chosen for working purposes..

Let me stress three points:

1. We should discard the old, unquestioned assumption that demographical always the best way of looking at markets.

The demographic premise implies that differences in reasons for buying bran choice influences, in frequency of use, or in susceptibility to be reflected in differences in age, sex, income, and geographical region. But this is usually not true. Markets should be scrutinized for important differences in buyer attitudes, motivations, values, usage pattern, sesthetic preferences, or degree of susceptibility. These may have demographic correlatives. Above all, we must never assume in advance that we know the best way of looking at a market. This is the cardinal rule of segmentation analysis. All ways of segmentation markets must be considered, and them we must select out of the various methods available the ones that have the most important implications for action, this process of choosing the strategically most useful mode of segmentation in the essence of the marketing approach espoused in this article.

In considering cases like those described, we must understand that we are not dealing with different types of people, but with differences in people's values. A women who buys a refrigerator because it is the cheapest available may want to buy the most expensive towels. A Ford-owner Kellogg's Corn Flakes-eater may be closed off to Chevrolet but sustainable to Post Toasties; he is the same man, but he has had different experiences and holds different values toward each product he purchases segmenting markets on the basis of the values, purposes, needs, and attitudes relevant to the product being studied, we are misleading information derived from attempts to divide people into type.

2. The strategic-choice concept of segmentation broadens the scope marketing planning to include the positioning of new products as well of established products.

It also has implications for brand planning, not just for individual products but for the composition of a line of competing brands where any meaningful segment in the market can possibly support a brand. One explanation of he successful competing brand strategy of companies like Procter & Gamble is that they are base don sensitivity to the many different modes of market segmentation. The brands offered by P & G often appear very similar to the outsider, but small, marginal differences between them appeal to different market segments. It is this rather than intramural competition that supports P&G successes.

3. Marketing must develop its own interpretive theory, and not borrow a ready-made one from the social sciences.

Marketing research, as an applied science, is tempted to borrow its theoretical structures from the discipline from which it derives. The socio sciences offer an abundance of such structures, but they are not applicable to marketing in their pure academic form. While the temptation to apply them in that form is great, it should be resisted. From sociology, for example, marketing has frequently borrowed the concept of status. This is a far-reaching concept, but it is not necessarily the most important one in a marketing problem, nor even one of the important ones. Again, early psychoanalytic theory has contributed an understanding of the sexual factor. While this can sometimes be helpful in an analysis of buying behaviour in a given situation, some motivation researchers have become oversensitive to the role of sex and, as a result, have made many mistakes. Much the same might be said of the concept of social character, that is, seeing the world as being "inner-directed," "other-directed," "tradition-directed," "autonomous," and so forth.

One of the values of segmentation analysis is that, while it has drawn on the insights of social scientists, it has developed an interpretive theory within marketing. It has been homegrown in business. This may explain ability to impose patterns of meaning on the immense diversity of the market, and to provide the modern marketing director with a systematic method for evolving true marketing objectives.

Product Differentiation and Market Segmentation as Alternative Marketing Strategies

Product differentiation efforts attempt to control demand through the promotion of product differences, while market segmentation efforts seek control by discovering, and responding to different product preferences. Success in deciding a product and services mix requires the use of both product differentiation and market segmentation as components of marketing strategy. The relationship of the strategies in imperfectly competitive markets in discussed.

Product differentiation and market segmentation are both consistent with the framework of imperfect competition. In its simplest product differentiation is concerned with the depending of demand to this will of supply. It is an attempt to shift or to change the slope of the demand curve for the market offering of an individual supplier. The strategy may also be employed by a group of suppliers such as a fare cooperative, the members of which have agreed to act together. It revels from the desire to establish a kind of equilibrium in the market brining about adjustment of market demand to supply conditions favourable to the seller.

Segmentation is based upon developments on he demand side of the market and represents a rational and more precise adjustment of product and marketing effort to consumer or user requirements. In the language the economist, segmentation is disaggregative in its effects and tends to bring about recognition of several demand schedules where only one was recognized before.

Attention has been drawn to this area of analysis by the increasing number of cases in which business problems have become soluble by doing something about marketing programmes and product policies that over generalize both markets and marketing effort. These are situations where intensive promotion designed to differentiate the company's products was to accomplishing its objective—cases where failure to recognize the reality of market segments was resulting in loss f market position.

While successful product differentiation will result in giving the marketer a horizontal share of a broad and generalized market, equally successful Application of

The strategy of market segmentation tends to produce depth of market position in the segments that are effectively defined and penetrated. The differentiator seeks to secure a layer of the market cake, whereas one who employs market segmentation strives to secure one or more wedge-shaped pieces.

Many examples of market segmentation can be cited; the

cigarette and automobile industries are well-known illustrations. Similar developments exist in greater or lesser degree in almost all product areas Recent introduction of a refrigerator with no storage compartment for frozen foods was in response to the distinguishable preference of the segment of the refrigerator market made up of home freezer owners who frozen food storage needs had already been met.

Strategies of segmentation and differentiation may be employed simultaneously, but more commonly they are applied in sequence in response to changing market conditions. In one sense, segmentation is a momentary of short-term phenomenon in that effective use of this strategy may lead to more formal recognition of the reality of market segments through redefinition of the segments as individual markets. Redefinition may result in a swing back to differentiation.

The literature of both economics and marketing abounds in formal definitions of product differentiation. From a strategy viewpoint, product differentiation is securing a measure of control over the demand for a product by advertising or promoting differences between a product and he products of competing sellers. It is basically the result of sellers' desires to establish firm market positions and/or to insulate their businesses against price competition. Differentiation tends to be characterized by heavy use of advertising and promotion and to result in prices that are somewhat above the equilibrium levels associated with perfectly compatible market conditions. It may be classified as a promotional strategy of approach to marketing.

Market segmentation, on the other hand, consists of viewing a heteroneous market (one characterized by divergent demand as a number of smaller homogeneous markets in response to differing product preferences among important market segments. It is attributable to the desires of consumers or users for more precise satisfaction of their varying wants. Like differentiation, segmentation often involves substantial use of advertising and promotion. This is to inform market segments of the availability of goods or services produced for or presented as meeting their needs with precision. Under these circumstances, prices tend to be somewhat closer to perfectly competitive equilibrium. Market segmentation is essentially a merchandising strategy, merchandising being used here in its technical sense as presentation the adjustment of market offerings to consumer or user requirements.

The Emergence of the Segmentation Strategy

To a certain extent, mart segmentation may be regarded as a force in the market that will not be denied. It may result from trial and error in the sense that generalized programmes of product differentiation may turnout to be effective in some segments of the market and ineffective in other. Recognition of, and intelligent response to, such as situation necessarily involves a shift in emphasis. On the other hand, it may develop that products involved in marketing programmes designed for particular market segments may achieve a broader acceptance than originally planned, that products involved in marketing programmes designed for particular market segments may achieve a broader acceptance than originally planed, thus revealing a basis for convergence of demand and a more generalized marketing approach. The challenge to planning arises from the importance of determining, preferably in advance, the level or degree of segmentation that can be exploited with profit.

There appear to be many reasons why formal recognition of market segmentation a a strategy is beginning to emerge. One of the most important of these is decrease in the size of the minimum efficient producting or manufacturing unit required in some product areas. American industry has also established the technical base for product diversity by gaining release from some of the rigidities imposed by earlier approaches to mass production. Hence, there is les need today for generalization of markets in response to the necessity for long production runs of identical items.

Present emphasis upon the minimizing of marketing costs through self-service and similar developments tends to impose a requirement for better adjustment of products to consumer demand. The retailing structure, in its efforts to achieve improved efficiency, is providing less and less sales push at point of sale. This increases the premium placed by retiles upon products that are pre sold by their producers and are readily recognized by consumers as meeting their requirements as measured by satisfactory rates of stock turnover.

It has been suggested that the present level of discretionary buying power is productive of sharper shopping comparisons, particularly for item that are above the need level. General prosperity also creates increased willingness "to pay a little more' to get "just what wanted."

Attention to market segmentation has also been enhanced by the recent ascendancy of product competition to a position of great economic importance. An expanded array of goods and services is competing for the consumer's dollar. More specially, advancing technology is creating competition between new and traditional materials with reference to metable construction materials, textile products, and in many other areas. While such competition is confusing and difficult to analyze in its early stages, it tends to achieve a kind of balance as various competing materials find their markets of maximum potential as a result of recognition of differences in the requirements of market segments.

Many companies are reaching the stage in their development where attention to market segmentation may be regarded as a condition or cost of growth. Their core markets have already been developed on a generalized basis to the point where additional advertising and selling expenditures are yielding diminishing returns. Attention to smaller or fringe market segments, which may have small potentials individually but are of crucial importance in the aggregate, may be indicated.

Finally, some business firms are beginning to regard an increasing share of their total costs of operation as being fixed in character. The higher costs of maintaining market position in the channels of distribution illustrate this change. Total reliance upon a strategy of product differentiation under such circumstances is undesirable, since market share available as a result of such a promotion-oriented approach tends to be variable over time. Much may hinge, for example, upon week-to-week audience ratings of the television shows of competitors who seek o out differentiate each other. Exploitation of market segments, which provides for greater maximization of consumer or user satisfactions, tends to build a more secure market position and to lead to greater over-all stability. While traditionally, high fixed costs (regarded primarily from the production viewpoint) have created pressures for expanded sale of standardized items through differentiation, the possible shifting of certain marketing costs into the fixed are a of the total cost structure tends to minimize this pressure.

Conclusion

Success in planning marketing activities requires precise utilization of both product differentiation and market segmentation as components of marketing strategy. It is fortunate that available techniques of marketing research make unplanned market exploration largely unnecessary. It is the obligation of those responsible for sales and marketing administration to keep the strategy mix in adjustment wit market structure at any point in time and to produce in marketing strategy at least as much dynamism as is present in the market. The ability of business to plan in this way is dependent upon the maintenance of a flow of market information that can be provided by marketing research as well as the full utilization of available techniques of cost accounting and cost analysis.

18

THEORY ON PRINCIPLES AND PRACTICES IN DEFENSE MARKETING

The Development of Defense is the largest single customers of American business. To be successful in the defense market, firms must recognize an adapt to the basic structure of the defense industry environment. Seven key factors in this environmental structure are discussed. A theory for organization of the defense marketing function is presented.

The defense industry has not been able to diversify successfully commercial practice. A central reason is its reported lack of marketing conversely, its fixation on the technical aspects of the firm. Defense marketing practices are:

1. No marketing concept at all
2. Shotgun proposals
3. Speaking to yourself
4. Loss of customers pulse
5. The contract firehose
6. Horse trading and browbeating
7. No time

The intent of this chapter is to suggest alternatives that might partially remedy the weaknesses noted above. Structurally, the paper consists of three segments: (1) the significant environmental factors, (2) a theory on defense marketing organisational activities, and (3) concepts and principles for marketing practice.

The objectives of marketing are reasonably independent of the specific environment of a firm. They relate to maximizing long-run profit through the provision of value (goods and services) to the customer. However, specific activities relating to the achievement of marketing objectives are a function of basic environmental factors. Thus, prior to presenting the conceptual organization the significant environmental factors are evaluated. Within this context specific marketing activities are recommended. And finally, specific broad guidelines or principles for marketing practices are offered.

Environmental Factors

Scope

The defense industry is one of the largest industries in the world. Approximately 8-10% of the gross national product is allocated to the seeds of he Department of Defense. About one-half of these dollars support the procurement of supplies and services. Total major military procurement actions fall in three areas: technical equipment items, services and non-equipment items. Technical equipment items consist of aircraft, missiles, ships, tanks, weapons, ammunitions, and electronics and communications equipment; and non-equipment items relate to subsisted textiles, clothing and equipage, fuels and lubricants, miscellaneous items account for over 70% of the allocated dollars. On the basis of corporate ownership, over 50% of defense contracts on a prime basis are allocated yearly to only four states—California, Texas, New York and Massachusetts. This does not reflect the impact of sub-contracting which is substantial. Major defense companies often sub-contract between 40-50% of the contract dollar. However, in many instances the major sub-contracting segments are other major defense contractors. Although large defense weapon contractors predominate in the defense business small business participation averages about 20%. Nevertheless, its participation in the defense contract industry is limited: 2.7% for aircraft, 12% for missiles, and about 10% for electronics.

The participation of small business is primarily in the non-technical category. In addition to military contracts, military installations in the United States account for a government, military, and civilian payroll of about $11 billion a year; and although this has been cut down recently by the actions of Defense Secretary McNamara, the payroll alone is still equal to one and one-half times the combined payrolls of iron and steel industry and all other basic metal producers, and is more than double the payroll of the automobile industry.

Zero Risk Conflict

What risk is the nation willing to take that Russia may establish military superiority. How many dollars must be spent to preclude this possibility At present, this country commits about 8% of its GNP to the Department of Defense. What role does cost reduction play when viewed from this perspective?

Created Competition

The environment is artificial – created by the Department of Defense. The building blocks of this created competition environment include: (1) Classifications of Research and development, (2) Programme definitions, (3) New Management Control systems such s PERT, and (6) Weighted Guide line Profit determination. The objective is to simulate an economic environment where competition will assure (1) a reasonable price and (2) incentive to provide quality on a timely basis.

The Real Product—Research and Development

The national science Foundation reports that 58% of the Reserves and Development Expenditures of industry were financed by the federal government in 1964 and that 90 per cent of this was attributed to the department of Defense and NASA. Hence, approximately 52% of the industry research and development is performed for defense space purposes.

Change and Obsolescence

Technical information is increasing at an increasing rate. It is not uncommon due to long lead times n development cycles that items finally readied for production are also ready for obsolescence. Defense firms must be able to adapt to rapid changes in demand.

One-hundred companies and their subsidiaries account annually for 70 per cent or more of defense procurement dollars. The twenty largest over companies alone receive over 50 per cent. Sub-contracting is substantial, but a good part goes to other large firms numbered among the top 100. When the companies are grouped by product, only a handful of companies are seriously considered for any given contract award. This is particularly true for large systems.

Quasi-Legalistic Structure

About 80 to 90 per cent of defense dollars each year flow to industry through the mechanism of the negotiation process and the vehicle of the procurement contract. A unique and specific body of government contract law exists to which defense marketing must adapt. It is far more rigorous than the legal restrictions of commercial marketing practices. The contract entered into by both parties describes and defines specific performance for almost all aspects of the business. And the government is foreign. The balance of power in the long run weights heavily toward the Sovereign Power – the Federal Government.

Political Eyeball

The Department of Defense and the defense industry play their game is a stadium where the seats are filled with representatives of our political system. Each spectator has his favorite team. The Labour Surplus and small business "set asides clauses" compound the problem. The federal government influences our economic system principally by indirect means. The defense expenditures offer an excellent vehicle for direct input. This economic tool is of vital interest to the political body. It is an area that has been evaluated objectively to date.

Theory on Defense Marketing Organizational Activities

An organization reflects the needs of the situation. Although there are many different approaches that could be effective for a given situation, a conceptual model or framework of reference is indispensable. It is important to have a way of thinking about marketing. From the conceptual model, adaptation can be made to varying circumstances.

An analysis of the defense environment suggests the following, (See Figure 1.)

Figure 1

Basic Marketing Functions

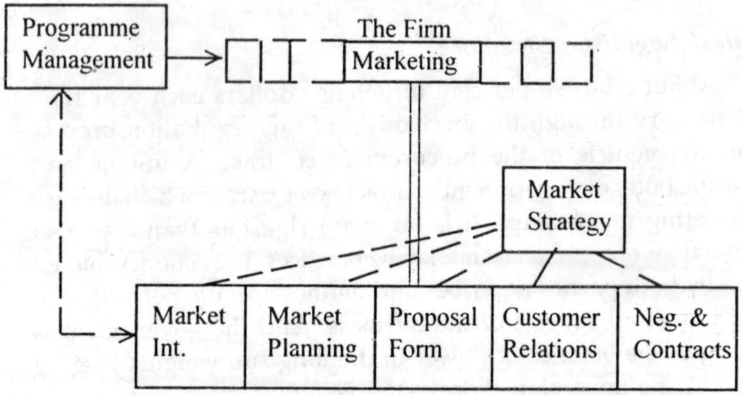

Basic Functions include: Engineering, Material, Marketing, Operations, Quality, Customer Relations, and Controller.

The major marketing activities are:

1. *Market Intelligence*—Information of a technical or general nature which contributes to improving a firm's competitive position.
2. *Market Planning*—The analysis of market intelligence data, the evaluation of alternative courses of action, the

establishment of target markets, and the development of marketing strategies related thereto.

3. *Proposal formulation*—The personal sales activity.
4. *Customer relations*—The personal sales activity.
5. *Negotiation*—The final phase of the selling process—the close. It is the determination by mutual agreement of the specific contractual terms and conditions under which the work is to be performed.

Market Intelligence

Contract award is highly correlated with (1) the firm that sells the initially to the government, and (2) the firm that finds out about the requirement before his competitors. Thus the importance of market intelligence is obvious. The need becomes particularly apparent when viewed in the context of the environment discussed earlier. The facets that the most dominant in shaping market intelligence needs are (1 orientations research and development, (2) change and obsolescence, (3) the competition, and (4) the political eyeball.

Market intelligence is derive from data from many sources (1) customer requirements, (2) procurement awards, (3) Federal statistics (4) Congressional and Senatorial hearings, (5) political contracts, (6) military contracts, (7) competitive firms, (8) commercial publications, and (9) customer relations.

Market intelligence to be effective should be an integral unit of the marketing team. Indeed, it is the rock upon which success sands or falls. It must be a formal organization entity directed toward specific marketing goals. Marketing intelligence forms the basis for new goals and/or the revision of existing targets. Intelligence cannot be a haphazard non-goal sciented function and be effective. Where scope warrants, effective utilization can be made of the computer and quantitative analysis techniques. This provides a criterion for rapid impact analysis of new data and its potential implications.

Market Planning

The task of market planning is to define marketing goals

and the means of their accomplishment. It relates to the development of marketing strategies and the variables to be considered in achieving the stated objectives. The Market Planning group should provide for the organization a of targets ranked according to their significance to the organization and the probability of award. This will require analysis of each specific requirement situation: Technical aspect, special facilities or know-how, competition, follow-on contracts, type of contract, time cycle. These factors are then compared with a critical self-examination to establish a probability of award for each contract. The probability of multiplied by the value to the organization provide the criteria for back.

If an intuitive evaluation leads to a different criterion, and inconsistency sales in the assignment of probabilities of ward, the values assigned or such.

Proposals should be written to specific people and should be directed toward a particular target contract. The customer relations actively aids in orienting the proposal to the needs and wants of the decision changed. Too often proposals are written in a vacuum and the firms' orientation itself;--i.e., talking to yourself.

Figure 2

	Profit	*Probability of Award*	*1 × 2*
Contract !	100	20	2000
Contract B	90	40	3600
Contract C	70	80	5600
Contract D	80	30	2400
Contract D	30	100	3000
Rank C, B, E, D,A.			

The proposal formulation activity should be a formal, permanent organizational unit rather than an ad hoc committee that needs after receive of requests for bid. It should participate in the market planning function through the market strategy committee. It works closely with customer relations to assure a rapport with the buyer. The guide for its activities the overall market strategy plan.

The growth and importance of the proposal activity is directly related to defense marketing environmental factors. The predominant factors (1) the emphasis of research and development, (2) created comparative (3) the quasi-legalistic orientation, and (4) the oligopolistic nature of supply function.

Customer Relations

Customer relations personnel develop the framework within which develop the proposal. One of the basic tasks is to cultivate a computer relationship with the decision channel. Thus it provides to the proposal group the orientation based on the needs, the personalities, the idiosynsies, and the receptiveness of the customer.

Customer relations must be cognizant of and participate in the over market strategy plan. It is then oriented to specific tasks and plays significant role in the execution, implementation, and feedback of established strategy.

Too often customer relations personnel are "charm Boys," Too of these "charm Boys" are loosely knit, non-directed group of geographically distributed representatives that operate in a vacuum apart form firm and distinct from the organization of which presumably they are a part.

Negotiation

Negotiation is the process by which mutual agreement is reached on conflicting positions. It is significant because since 1950 between 80 and 90 per cent of dollars have flowed to the defense industry through the process of negotiation. Negotiation, unfortunately, is often characterized by loss of customer pulse, the contract fire those, horse trading, and browbeating. The following is offered as an approach to the Negotiation Process in lieu of the above.

Figure 3

The Negotiation Process*

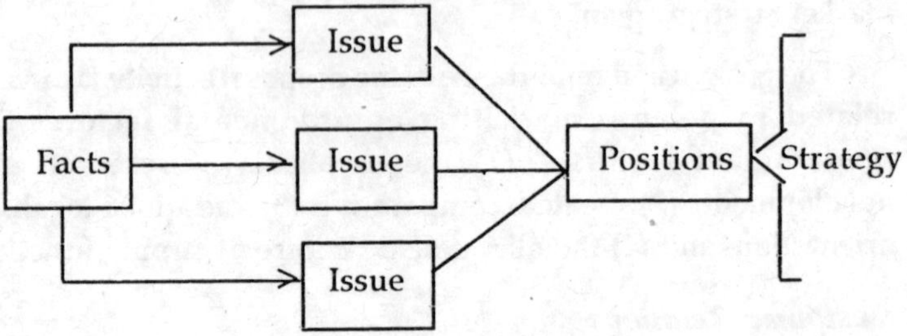

Facts: 1. Classify by issue and strategy

2. Catalog by degree and method of supportability

Issues: 1. Rank of importance

2. Use-non-use

3. Catalog for strategy use

4. Real-apparent

Positions: 1. Classified by importance

2. Facts cataloged by issue and related to positions

3. Maximum, minimum ad target positions

Strategy: 1. Analysis of procurement situation

2. Analysis of procurement situation

3. Positions

4. Human behaviour

5. Timing

6. Organization

* John J. Kennedy, "the negotiation Process," unpublished paper, University of Notre Dame.

Negotiation, when viewed as a process, includes the variables of objectives, facts, issues, positions, strategy, and human behavior.

These must be viewed in the context of the specific procurement situation. Te management of the negotiation process relates to the planning, organizing controlling of these variables to maximize long-range corporate objectives.

The first step in a successful negotiation is to determine specific goals based on the factors prevalent for the given procurement. Facts are gathered and analyzed, Issues are identified through this analysis and the facts are then cataloged by issue. Issues are potential areas of disagreement that could preclude the accomplishment of the goals. The facts are classified by issue to facilitate the development of positions. Positions represent the companies stand on the issues.

In the development of positions, the company must identify areas of possible agreement. Toward this end it is advisable that the range include maximum, minimum, and target positions. Facts, issues, and positions must then be woven into strategies.

Te strategy is a function of the objectives, the positions based on faces and issues, and the other facets of the procurement situation. These include competition, follow-on contracts, current capacity, past experience, and the personnel involved. Strategy is also closely associated with a knowledge of human behaviour. Although it is not within the context of this paper to explore this area in depth, the following reflects its role is the negotiation process.

WE respond to honest praise and dislike criticism. This is a cornerstone of every sales kit out too often it is ignored. Most of us will let the other fellow lead – this can be important. It is often advisable to grasp the rein to guide the session. Leading often facilitates strategy implementation. You don't always change a person's mind with facts; human beings tend to interpret facts as necessary to preconceived ends. Once a pattern of decision making is established, it ends to persist. Therefore, start that negotiation session positively. Get off to a good start.

The marketing functions thus are pars of a whole – the fingers on hand that work in rhythm and unison with a common goal. The following will assist the reader in the relationship of these functions to their environment.

Guides to Marketing Practices

Principles are statements of truth applicable under most conditions. The following represent a distillation of the ideas growing out of Parts and II of this paper. They, of course, are not principles tested by through research; rather, they emerge as probable guides t action that must be adapted to specific circumstances.

1. Defense products must be sold.
2. Success in obtaining contracts, assuming previous good performance, is directly related to: (a) demand creation, (b) the level of propose sophistication, (c) cultivation of the decision chain, (d) the expertise of the customs relations

FIGURE 4

The Defense Marketing Function and Its Environment

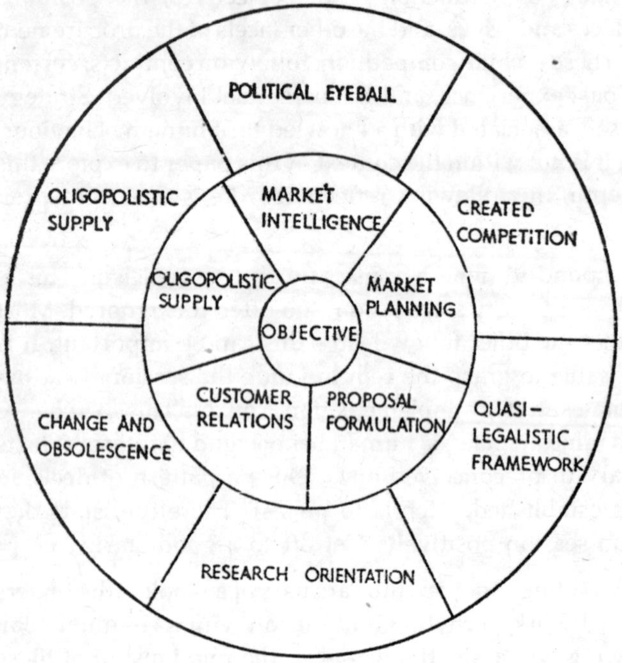

function, and (e) the extent to which some market planning has been undertaken based on market intelligence.

3. A company cannot successfully ignore the government's role as sovereign. The government will win most arguments over the long run.
4. There is a definite correlation between the image of the company is the minds of those in the decision channel and the company's success in obtaining defense contracts.
5. The smaller the company and the more highly specialized its product, the greater the price flexibility.
6. An outstanding proposal will contribute to a capable company's dances for contract award. However, an outstanding proposal will not help a company whose image with a decision channel is highly negative.
7. Proposals have to be written for a specific purpose and oriented to specific individuals in the decision channel.
8. Prior knowledge of negotiation and its principle sand theories and ability to apply them is generally more important than specific product knowledge.
9. Satisfactory performance over a long period of time is not sufficient to warrant success in the defense market. The defense market can be impersonal as you want it to be. Conversely, it can be as impersonal as let it be.
10. A defense company organization is directly affected by the organizational philosophy of the customer.
11. Proposals are advertising; they must be planned and budgeted.
12. A dominant factor that can cause marketing success or failure is the ability to adapt to sudden shifts in the demand patterns of the customer.

Conclusion

The defense market is one of the largest in the world. Basic environmental factors include: nature of product, emphasis on research and development, oligopolistic nature of supply, political interests and reactions, quasi-legalistic structure, and sovereign power concept.

Organizations can be analyzed from many different bases. A functional analysis provides an insight into the nature of the activities that art required for performance. Activities tend to group according to commonality of problems, necessary tools for solution of problems, knowledge of skills required, and so on. Thus the organization reflected suggests the certain basic functions or activities have emerged in the defense marketing environment. And these functions, as would be expected, are reactions to and are both cause and effect of the general and specific environment forces. The basic functions are market intelligence, market planning proposal formulation, customer relations, and negotiation and contract. These functions are coordinated and directed by the market strategy and general plan which details specific goals and their means of accomplishment.

The marketing task is to anticipate needs of the consumer and provide such needs as effectively and efficiently as possible in accordance with overall corporate objectives. The marketing activities and practices related to the task vary wit the environment; but nevertheless exist Defense marketing needs exist. A framework of reference for the defense marketing sphere is the prerequisite.

19

THE ART' OF MARKETING THEORY

Assessing the "state of the art" of marketing theory is at best a difficult task. Marketing theory is not a well-categorized and orderly collection of substantive ideas, concepts, hypotheses, and generalizations. It has not resulted form orderly inquiry and development, resulted from orderly inquiry and development, nor has it provided a cumulative summation and framework of marketing knowledge. Rather, marketing theory is comprised of a haphazard array of research findings, published and unpublished manuscripts, philosophical constructs and speculations, and untested hypotheses from a wide variety of sources concerning a road and complex spectrum of topics related to marketing.

Marketing theory has often been used by those interested in the more practical aspects of marketing to mean the opposite of factual, useful, or practical, sometimes it is used to connote the lack of evidence, or universified hypothetical speculation. ("That's all right in theory.") Bt marketing theory is not "pure" theory in the sense of being only hypothetical and philosophic. Rather it is applied, theory. It is concerned with reality, problem solving, polices, gaining factual information, and developing useful principles and bodies of knowledge. Marketing theory must have an empirical footing and be tested on a pragmatic basis.

The masterworks of marketing theory are not to be fund in marketing textbooks. They are still to be developed. Marketing theory is not a heritage all laid out; it is a vital, viable, emerging area.

A good proportion of marketing literature is descriptive. The description of marketing activities and accumulation of observations, however, is important to marketing theory. It is only through the progress of specialized research. And the assembly of marketing facts and information, that marketing becomes recognized as a self-supporting subject matter entity, and marketing thought develops.

Marketing thought, nevertheless, cannot proceed merely by the accumulation of observations unregulated by theory. Fruitful observations cannot be made, nor their results ordered and correlated, without the use of hypotheses which go beyond the existing state of knowledge. The development of marketing theory does not merely require stockpiling of facts upon facts. Yet much of the current literature consists of isolated fats and findings, which relate to restricted areas of interest, changing subjects, and limited spans of time. The problem of deriving generalizations from the facts, and relating generalizations by higher-order conceptual schemes is a critical one for marketing theory.

Purpose and Requisites of Marketing Theory

Purpose

The major purpose of marketing theory is to orderfacts so they facilitate the explanation, comprehension, and prediction of marketing phenomena. Maketign theory is concerned with generating postulates and theorems from which implications can be derived; establishing laws and principles which summarise empirical investigations and explain facts; and developing general theories which formulate propositions about universals.

The development of marketing theory will require the organization and unification of findings, the synthesis of theoretical and practical constructs, and an emphasis on the value of a theoretical perspective. Marketing theory should summate findings and hypotheses in such related areas as consumer behaviour, distribution channels, physical distribution, marketing planning, and the measurement of advertising effectiveness. It should systematize, integrate and relate marketing knowledge, and help provide a framework for analyzing and solving problems.

Practitioners in approaching marketing theory often expect to find direct answers to current problems – particularly research problems. When answers are not found, marketing theory is rejected as useless. However, the total purpose of marketing theory is not problem solving. A major function of marketing theory is to stimulate thought, and generate insight, understanding, hypotheses, and new theories.

The achievement of solutions, and the generation of information alone, are not enough to develop marketing science and to advance the marketing discipline. Abstractions as well as facts become important in explaining marketing phenomena.

Requisites

Two requisites for an adequate body of marketing theory are:

(1) The existence of an adequate and unified conceptual framework within which meaningful statements about marketing phenomena can be formulated this refers to the synthesis of facts, the search for universals, principles, laws and hypotheses, and the development of theories related to broad categories of marketing activity.

(2) The usefulness of these theoretical statements in explaining, interpreting and predicting marketing phenomena. This emphasizes the role of theory in understanding and solving marketing problems.

In general these criteria are not met, partly because marketing phenomena are intangible, vague and imperfectly observable. Much of the theoretical literature in marketing takes the form of descriptive, verbalistic essays, which lack clarity, precision, operational meaning, and verification, and which appeal to common sense intuitive understanding. Marketing is lacking in neat uniform theories derived from fundamental axioms, basic concepts, definitions, and theorems.

General Theories

General theories in marketing cannot be expected to provide theorems or principles that correspond exactly to specific research tasks. Marketing theory, however, should be expected to provide guides and directives for research and problem solving. It should serve as a point of reference for evaluating the significance and meaning of empirical evidence. It is not the province of marketing theory to state precisely what the impact of competitor A's ads will be when interacting with competitor B's ads. Rather, theory must focus on general questions, problems, and basic interpretations involving universals.

Questions have been raised in the literature about the necessity and possibility of developing a general theory of marketing. Many theorists seem to hold little promise for the development of a useful general theory of marketing. They seem to feel that because of the diversity and complexity of the subject matter, the large number of variables, and the dynamic nature of marketing phenomena, that rather than a general theory of marketing, a number of theories about specific aspects of marketing probably will be developed.

To date, we are a long way from a general system, or systems, of marketing theory. Much of the literature on marketing theory is comprised of imprecise, inoperable verbages. It is not comprised of axiomatic systems, hypothetical laws, principles, or theorems that can be tested. Many of the theoretical generalizations contained in the marketing literature seem to fall into the following categories:

(1) tautologies, truisms, or overly general statements that are of very limited use n developing marketing science;

(2) Specific statements that apply to a particular or unique case only;

(3) Statements which are directly in the realm of another discipline tangential or contiguous to marketing, such as

psychology, sociology, or anthropology.

Changing Focus of Marketing Theory

Marketing theory is now in a period of transition. It is reflecting the legitimization of the marketing discipline which is progressing rapidly. The process of legitimizing is evident in the increasing attention being directed to the societal aspects of marketing (marketing as the means of satisfying consumer wants and needs); the scientific methods of investigation that are being utilized; the basic models and paradigms that are being developed; and the concepts and theoretical findings from other disciplines that are being introduced.

Important Changes

Among the important changes occurring in the marketing discipline from the point of view of marketing theory are:

(1) Less reliance on the speculative, intuitive approach to marketing;

(2) The recognition and emancipation marketing is seeking as a science;

(3) The expansion of the concept of marketing from one of sales, or of institutions, to include marketing as a pervasive force in the firm as a whole, in our economic system and competitive environment, in our society, and in world-affairs and markets;

(4) The de-emphasis of the introspective concern with description and classification;

(5) Concentration on marketing decision making, marketing planning, and marketing systems;

(6) Placement of marketing under the same rigorous methods as other scientific disciplines such as physics, chemistry, sociology, and psychology.

The decade of the 1920's has been labeled the "golden decade" in the development of marketing because of the integration, classification, refinement, and development of marketing thought, as well as the publication of principles textbooks. For the development of marketing theory, however, the period since 1941, particularly the postwar years, have the greatest significance and the most relevance. Most of the major articles, books, and doctoral dissertations in the theory are have appeared since that time.

Two Extremes

Two extremes in the development of marketing theory seem to be suggested; descriptive factualism and generalism. Marketing theory seems to be moving away form the extreme end of descriptive factualism toward the development of general principles and theories. It also seems to be progressing from classical behaviouralism which emphasized descriptive accounts of institutional behaviour toward functionalism. The latter emphasizes the adjustive and adaptive aspects of behaviour, the interaction and adjustment of the business with the external environment, and the linkage of marketing and corporate success with consumer behaviour.

To a considerable extent, marketing theory has been rooted in descriptive empiricism and factualism, that in general seem to approach Baron's process of simple enumeration. Facts have been stressed more than generalizations, principles or laws. Generalizations and theories are challenged on the basis of lack of correspondence with particular events in reality—the practical. Static descriptions, definitions, and categorization seem to be especially characteristic of the theoretical material prior to the war. Dynamic theories, quantitative models, and probabilistic reasoning have been introduced in the theoretical writings after the war.

Shift in Approach and Method

Marketing theory has witnessed a shift in both approach and method. There has been a shift form subjective intuitive approaches to objective, more formalize approaches to theory (models, mathematics, statistics); from the qualitative to the quantitative, even in "unlikely" areas, of attitudes, opinions, and motivations (scaling and projective techniques); from rigorous classifications to gradations and refinements; from classification to causation; from static to dynamic theories; from disjointed facts and descriptions to a search for generalizations, principles, theories, and laws; from surface analysis to depth investigations; from sheer speculation (which is necessary) to realism and more directly applicable concepts and theories.

Marketing Theory, Marketing Science, and Marketing Technology

Marketing scientists and marketing technologists or clinicians differ in their emphasis. Theory building is one of the primary focuses of marketing scientists. Problem solving is the major concern of the technologist or clinician. Yet, the domain of each is overlapping.

Marketing theory and marketing science are linked inextricably. Like marketing theory, marketing science is concerned with classified and systematized bodies of marketing knowledge that tare organized around central theories, laws, principles, and concepts, which permit prediction (and sometimes control), and which often may be expressed in quantitative terms.

Marketing theory is the handmaiden of marketing science. It also is one of the goals of marketing science. It is the goal of marketing science, since science tries to explain as much of reality as possible in the form of generalizations than permit prediction. Marketing theory, in fact, it validated by its capacity to predict marketing behaviour and consequences under specified conditions. Its foundation is controlled observation of the real world and verifiable hypothetical speculations.

Marketing theorists and marketing technologists or clinicians have common tasks and concerns. As a result of technologists' research and problem solving activities, masses of facts have been accumulated about various aspects of marketing for specific companies, products, industries, and techniques. The marketing theorist needs more practical facts and knowledge upon which to base generalizations and test hypotheses and theories. The practitioner requires more orderly knowledge about marketing phenomena as guides to action and aids in prediction. This is not necessarily the case in other social or behavioural sciences.

For instance, in the field of learning theory, or perception, the psychologist tends to rely almost exclusively upon his experiments rather than checking the predictable consequences of conclusions by happenings in the real world. In marketing, however, it appears that experience and factual observations provide the major opportunities for theory construction. Marketing theory seems to be experimentally, rather than experimentally, rather than experimentally based. Currently, some tendency toward the experimental may be noted.

Perhaps it is meaningful and helpful to distinguish two kinds of theory in marketing: scientific theory and clinical or technical theory. Scientific theories are concerned with the development of generalizations that link together unique and distinct theoretical formulations about marketing into more general theories constructs. Clinical or technical theories are those marketing theories that have prescription, or problem solving, as their major emphasis.

The distinction drawn is not absolute. However, it points up he direct linkage in marketing between the theoretical and the pragmatic. Both are necessary for a better understanding of marketing and the development of marketing theory and marketing science.

Lack of Theoretical Emphasis

Theory has been a neglected area of marketing. It has been neglected by both the academicians and practioners. Facts and descriptions have been stressed. Emphasis has been given to what is, rather than to theoretical foundations of what is.

Lack of Theorists

Marketing unfortunately has never had theorists as have the fields of physics, mathematics, statistics, economics, and sociology: The latter disciplines accord the highest rating and stature to theoreticians. Theorists are usually recognized as masters of their professions—they are valued and esteemed. This is not the case in marketing. The practitioner, the technicians, the researcher, and problem-solver, who implement techniques and concepts in practical situations, seem to receive the greatest acclaim in marketing. Theory tends to be skirted and ignored.

Institutions Neglect Theory Courses

The lack of theoretical emphasis in marketing, even in academic institutions, is readily evidenced. The Marketing Science Institute recently conducted a survey of marketing theory courses offered at the graduate level in schools of business. A survey was taken by mail of 181 graduate schools offering courses in marketing. They were asked about "marketing theory courses" offered and the books and periodicals used in the course. Of 53 responses received, only 24 course offerings in either marketing theory or the development of marketing thought were reported. Another 28 schools reported that they offered "some theory in their seminars and courses."

From the results of the survey it would appear that the desirability of offering "marketing theory curses" is recognized by graduate schools of business. The actual courses, however, have been neglected. Many f the answers received revealed a rather defensive attitude toward the lack of theory courses. A large proportion of the answers expressed the thought that, "while we don't have a curse in marketing theory specifically, we cover theory in our courses on..."

The list of material used in courses described as "theory curses" ranged from basic textbooks and case books (hardly theoretical sources), to books on inventory control and readings in journals of related disciplines.

It is reasonable to expect that marketing as a discipline taught at the graduate level should emphasize theoretical content. A common core of concepts, generalizations, and areas of study might be anticipated. This, however, is not the case. Current perceptions of theoretical material are extremely varied. Common theoretical, denominators for marketing theory courses seem to be lacking.

Interest in Theory Increases

Despite the lack of the theoretical accomplishment in marketing, interest in theory seems to be increasing. Since 1950 greater emphasis ha been given to books, monographs, and articles relating to marketing theory. Several doctoral dissertations have been written on the general subject of marketing theory. The informal, invitational Marketing Theory seminar has recently received more than passing attention by marketing scholars. It appears that the long overdue recognition of the importance and necessity of developing marketing theory is at last emerging.

To date, however, the most theoretical aspects of marketing seem to be constructs associate with demand analysis and pricing under various market conditions are examples. This is not unexpected since economics is the parent discipline of marketing. Marketing emerged at a time when the institutional approach to economics was developing and the fundamental and direct theoretical contributions of economics are still underscored. Increasingly, however, emphasis is being given to the contributions of disciplines other than economics to the development of marketing theory. They will become more significant in the future.

Approaches to Marketing Theory

Marketing theory has no schools of thought to parallel those existing in other disciplines. For example, the marketing equivalent of gestalt, Behavioural, or Clinical schools of psychology does not exist. The marketing literature contains no burning debates about the superiority of one approach, emphasis, or group of concepts to others. The closest approach to a school of thought in marketing is functionalism as developed by Alderson, which examines the way in which organized marketing group function in the continuous adjustment to an operating environment.

Interdisciplinary Approach

The interdisciplinary approach to marketing is receiving increasing attention and is shaping theoretical contributions. It recognizes the theoretical and conceptual contributions of other disciplines in addition to economics. Both behavioural science and quantitative concepts are proving to be helpful in extending marketing theory. Concepts of social class, status, symbols, images, systems, and such quantitative models as linear programming, Markov process, and exponential smoothing are examples.

The interdisciplinary perspective broadens the theoretical horizon of marketing. It can offer classification and interchange of information and viewpoints, terms, concepts, findings, and hypotheses. By searching out and sifting common areas, findings are being fused, evidence accumulated, insights gained, and theoretical boundaries extended.

As the frontiers of marketing theory are pushed out they will permit increasing unification of marketing theory with other areas of theory. However, this will not result in a merging of disciplines at the conceptual level. Rather it is a matter of using the data and findings of disciplines for marketing insights. Marketing theory is supplemented by, but different from, sociological, psychological, and anthropological theory, Marketing has its own viewpoint and set of problems which circumscribe the parameters of marketing theory.

Early Approaches

Most of the early approaches to marketing theory ere theory were rather mechanistic in nature. Machine-types concepts and models that seem to parallel the concepts of classical mechanics were used. Various models of wholesale and retail institutions, selling formulas, pricing strategies, and advertising guides are examples. Recently, however, dynamic probabilistic concepts and techniques have been employed. The use of simulation. Markov models, game theory concepts, and Bayesian statistics are manifestations of a trend away from mechanistic approaches. Acceptance of probability concepts and approaches helps overcome criticism of the lack of exactness and the demand for complete correspondence between marketing theory and the real marketing world.

Quantitative and Behavioural Approaches

Quantitative and behavioural approaches seem to be accepted

as superior to the more traditional or classical approaches in constructing marketing theory. All marketing activity, however, is not quantifiable, nor does it fit the present molds of behavioural science concepts and theories. Even the tautological generalizations and truisms, which make up a good portion of the theory literature in marketing references, are useful. Description and classification of marketing activities along classical lines is both necessary and valuable. The traditional marketing approaches should not be cast aside because they are classical rather the framework presented should be enriched.

Conclusions

The exciting age in marketing theory is still to come. Marketing theorists are presently concerned with clarification, language, concepts, consolidation, and synthesis which my be a preview to a major attack on marketing theory. Unlike economics, psychology, and sociology, marketing has not felt the theoretical impact of a Keynes, Freud, of Parsons However, a feeling of greater intellectual excitement about theoretical aspects of various areas of marketing seems to exist.

BIBLIOGRAPHY

A.H. Maslow, *Motivation and Personality* (New York: Harper & Row, Publishers, 1954), pp. 80-106.

Arthur D. Hall, "A Methodology for Systems Engineering," (Toronto, Canada: Van Nostrand, 1962), p. 60.

Bakke, E. Wright, "concept of the Social Orgnization," General Systems, Vo. IV (1959), pp. 95-121.

Barach, Arnold B. "U.S.A. and Its Economci Future," Twentieth Century Fund Report. New York: Macmillan Co., 1964.

Baumol, William J. Business Behaviour, Value and growth, New York: Macmillan Co., 1959.

Buss, Perry, *Marketing and the Behavioural Science*, 2nd ed. Boston: Allyn and BCON, Inc., 1967.

Chandler, Alfred D., Jr. Strategy and Structure, Cambridge, Mass.: M.I.T. Press, 1962.

David M. Potter, People of Plenty, The University of Chicago Press, Chicago, 1954, p. 167.

B. Harper W., Jr., and Levy, Sidney J. "New Dimension in Consumer Analysis," *Harvard Business Rview*, Vol. XLI, NO. 6 (November-December, 1963), pp. 129-40.

Ernet. "Discovering the Inner Jones," *Harvard Busines Review*, Vol. XLIII, No. 3 (May-June, 1965), pp. 6 ff.

Eugene J. Kelley, "The Importance of Convenience in Consumer Purchasing," *Journal of Marketing*, July 1958. (Also reprinted in this book, pp. 155-62).

Fred J. Borch, "The Marketing Philosophy as a Way of Business Life," *Marketing Series* No. 99, American Management Association, 1957.

Ferrer, Robert, And Wales, Hugh, G. (eds). *Motvation and Market Behavoiur*, Homewood, Illinoois: Richard D. (rwin, Inc., 1958.

Festinger, L. A Theory of Cognitive Dissonaance, Stanford, Calif.: Stanford University Press, 1957.

George Katona, *Michigan Business Review*, July 161, pp. 17-20.

G. Charres Y. and Nicosia, Francesco M. "Uses of Sociology instudying ConsmptionBehaviour,*Journal of Marketing*, Vol. 28, No. 3 (July, 1964), pp. 51-54.

Gottman, J. "Megalopolis: The Urbanized Northeastern Seaboard of he U.S., "*Twentieth Century Fund Report*, New York: Macmillan Co., 1961.

Herman E. Koenig, "Theory of Modeling Socio-Economic Systems," mimeographed paper. Department of electrical Engineering, Michigan State University, p. 12.

James G. Drury, "Is Your Problem Overproduction—or Underproduction of Markets?" Printers' Ink, July 5, 1957, pp.19-22, 58.

J.L. Henderson, *The Order of Nature* (Cambridge, Mass: Harvard University Press, 1917), p. 172.

Jay W. Forrester, "Industrial Dynamics," Harvard Business Review, Vol. XXXVI, No. 4 (July-August, 1958), p. 52.

J.M. Clark, "Competition: Static Models and Dynamic Aspects," *American Economic Review*, Vol. XLV, No. 2, May 1955, p. 462.

Katona, George, "Rational Behaviour and Economic Behaviour," *Psychological Reveiw*, Vol. LX, No. 5 (September, 1953), pp. 307-18.

Katona, George, *The Powerful Consumer*. New York: McGraw-

Hill Book Co., Inc., 1960.

Kelley, Eugene, J. *Marketing: Strategy and Functions*. Englewood Cliffs, N.J.: Prntice-Hall, Inc., 1965.

Kelley, Eugene J.: Lazo,Hector: Corbin, Arold:and Kahn, Edward. *Marketing Management: An Annotated Biblioraphy*, Chicago: american Mrketing Associiton, 1963.

Konrad Lorenz, *On Aggression* (New York: Harcourt, Brace & World, Inc., 1966), p. xi.

Krcoman, H.e., andHartley, E.L. "The Learning of Tastes," *Public Opinion Quarterly*, Vol XXIV, No. 4 (Winter, 1960), pp. 621-31.

Louis Finkelstein in Conference On The American Character, *Bulletin, Center For The Study of Democratic Institutions*, October, 1861, p. 6.

Malineau, Pierre, "Social Class and Spending Behaviour," *Journal of Marketing*, Vol. 23, No. 2 (October, 1958), pp. 121-30.

Michael Kraus, "The United States to 1865," The University of Michigan Press, Ann Harbor, Michigan, 1959.

M. Francesco, Consumer Decision Processes: Marketign and Advertising Implicaitons, Englewood Cliffs, New Jersey:Prentie-Hall, Inc., 1966.

M. George, L.F., "The Socio-Economic Status of cities and Suburbs," *American Sociological Review*, Vol. XXVIII, No. 1 (February, 1963),pp. 14-85.

Neal, James U. *Dimension of Consumer Behaviour*. New York: Appleton-Century-Crofts, 1965.

Nelson Foote, "he Anatomy of the Consumer," in Lincoln H. Clark, ed. *Consumer Behaviour, The Dynamics of Consumer Reaction*, New York University Press, pp. 21.24.

Nelson N. Foote, "The Image of the Consumer in the Year 2000," Proceedings, Thirty-Fifth Annual Boston Conference on distribution, 1963, pp. 13-18.

O.R. Young, "A Survey of General Systems Theory," *General*

Systems, Vol. IX (1984), pp. 6-62.

Pitirim A. Sorokin, *The Crisis of Our Age*, New York, E.P. Dutton & Co., Inc., 1946, especially Chapter III.

Roger Girod, "Comment on Consumer Reaction to Innovation," In Lincoln H. Clark, ed. *Consumer Behavior, Research on Consumer Reactions*, Harper & Brothers, New York, 1958, p. 10.

Simonds, Rollin H.: Ball, Richard E.; and Kelley, Eugene J. Business Administration: PROBLEMS And Functions. Boston: Allyn and Bacon, Inc., 1962.

Stafford Beer, "What Has Cybernetics To Do With Operational Research?" *Operational Research Quarterly*, Vol. X, No. 1 (March, 1959), p. 3.

Tarpley, Lawrence X. "Marketign Resarch and the Behavioural Sciences," Business Topics, Vol. XIII, No. 1 (Winter, 1965), pp. 6-67.

Toynbee vs. Bernbach: As Advertising Morally Defensible?" *Yale Daily News*, Special Issue, 1963, p. 2.

Young, O.R. "A Survey of General Systems Theory," *General Systems* Vol. IX (1964, pp. 61-80.

William Lazer & Eugene . Kelley, "Editorial Postscript," *Managerial Marketing: Perspectives & Viewpoints* (rev. ed.; Hotnewood, III.: Richard D. Irwin, Inc., 1963), p. 683.

Wroe Alderson, "Advancing Marketing Efficiency," from the *Proceedings of the 41st National Conference of the American Marketing Association*, December, 1958.

Wroe Alderson, *Dynamic Marketing Behavior* (Homewood, III.: Richard D. Irwin, Inc., 1965), chap.1.

W. Fckwardy, "The Challenge of Megalopolis," *Twentieth Century Fund Report*. New York: Macmillan Co., 1964.

W.M.A. Brooker, "the Total Systems Myth," *Systems and Procedures Journal* (July-August, 1965), p. 29.